THE SIMPLE ART OF BUSINESS ETIQUETTE

THE

SIMPLE ART

of

BUSINESS

ETIQUETTE

HOW TO RISE
TO THE TOP BY
PLAYING NICE

JEFFREY L. SEGLIN

TYCHO
PRESS

For Evan, Lucas, Michaela, and Tess.

"Thus, I give up the spear!"

—from Herman Melville's *Moby Dick*

Contents

Acknowledgments

For the past 17 years, I've written a column called "The Right Thing" that focuses on ethics and business ethics. Along the way, I have had many editors and two or three different homes for the column. The work I've done on the column informs many of the examples included in this book. Thank you to the many editors of "The Right Thing," both those who directly worked with me on the column and those who worked on the column when it appeared in the various publications that carried it. A particular thanks to Jim Schachter, my original editor for the column when it ran in the Sunday *New York Times*, and now the vice president of news for WNYC.

The idea for this book came from Brian Hurley, senior managing editor at Callisto Media. It was Brian who was convinced I was the right person to write this book, and Brian who worked with me until he believed the manuscript was ready. Brian was also responsible in enlisting the services of Lauren O'Neal, who did a detailed line editing of the manuscript, and Peggy Paul, who copyedited the manuscript, Frances Baca, Katy Brown, and Felicia Reyes, who designed the book, Greg Johnson, who laid it out, Amy Boulanger, who wrote the copy, and Katerina Malone, who facilitated all of the above. Each of them made the book far better than I could have made it on my own. I particularly am indebted to Anna McCurdy, the person from Callisto who makes sure I get paid, because she made sure I got paid.

At Harvard, I owe thanks to Alison Kommer, the program coordinator for the communications program I direct at Harvard Kennedy School. Her efforts make the program better than it would be if left to my own devices.

My daughter, Bethany, offered me feedback on some material in the book that I found challenging to make as clear as possible.

Thanks to her, that stuff is now clear. Thank you as well to my son, Ed, son-in-law, David, and daughter-in-law, Lisa. John Waggoner and Loren Gary know what they did, and it's appreciated. At a moment when I needed her insight most, Lorraine Gatto rushed to the rescue, as lifesavers such as she are prone to do.

I have been quite fortunate to work with some amazing students at Emerson College and now at Harvard. Many of them think I'm kidding when I tell them that I get far more out of working with them than they get from working with me, but it's the truth. Their insight and curiosity help make me a better writer and, I hope, a better teacher.

Most everything I write that leaves the house is reviewed by my wife, Nancy, the woman I'd eat bees for. Nancy was my first book editor many years ago. She has since become a psychotherapist. In spite of the career change, Nancy still reads everything I write and gives me the most thoughtful feedback of any I receive. The good that she adds to our lives together goes far beyond her ability to recognize a comma splice.

Jeffrey L. Seglin
jseglin@post.harvard.edu

Introduction

Shortly after I left my full-time job as a magazine editor to start work as a college professor, my wife was driving me to my new office so I could drop off some boxes. On the car radio, one of the local stations was reporting on a new ethics and honesty poll from Gallup.

Among the top 10 professions that Americans found to be most honest and ethical was college professor, my new career. But before I could become too smug, the reporter announced that journalists—my old career—were in the bottom 10.

As a journalist who was joining the ranks of college professors, I found myself in a bit of a quandary. What do I tell people if I'm at a cocktail party and someone asks me what I do for a living? Do I give them the answer that will make them think I'm more honest and ethical? Or do I give them both answers and take a risk that they'll find only half of me to be trustworthy?

My wife reminded me that I don't go to cocktail parties, so it likely wouldn't be an issue.

But the momentary crisis made me think deeply about how I present myself in the workplace and how much other people's perceptions matter. Whether I am in a highly respected professional role or one that is a bit more suspect, it doesn't change who I am or how I behave. Right?

I want to do good work and to enable my colleagues to do good work as well. So I try to have as much respect for the job and my colleagues as I can. Sometimes this is simple. Other times, it's a challenge. But I never want to let those challenges cause me to become the type of person I swore I'd never become. I want to work with integrity. I want to appreciate others without letting workplace bullies run roughshod over me.

So far it's going pretty well. For years, I've written an ethics column, first monthly for the Sunday *New York Times*, then weekly for the *New York Times* Syndicate, and now weekly for Tribune Media. I'm an ethics fellow at the Poynter Institute for Media Studies. I'm a lecturer and a program director at the Harvard Kennedy School.

I wouldn't have accomplished any of this without making an effort to respect my colleagues. None of it would have been possible if I'd been a jerk to people.

I wrote this book to help you do what I did—what I keep trying to do on a daily basis, with some days turning out better than others. I want you to thrive in the workplace without losing your own identity. I want you to see how working well with others takes some effort—not too much effort, but some.

That's what business etiquette is. It's behaving appropriately even in awkward situations. It's learning how to handle conflict gracefully. It's recognizing that the workplace is not your rec room, but rather a place to do meaningful work with others. It's making sure you never forget who you are and why you wanted to do this kind of work in the first place. This book will help you see that you are constantly faced with a challenge. Can you achieve your desired result in a way that leaves your principles and your personal identity intact?

Each part of this book focuses on a specific type of challenge in the workplace, tells a story, and asks you to think about what you would have done if you were in someone else's shoes. Unless otherwise specified, the scenarios in this book do not use the names of real people, and the specifics of their situations may have been altered. But if I write about something *I* did, then I did indeed do it. If you recognize yourself or others in this book, it's only because I drew on years of experience with people's behavior at work. We've all met these people. Some of us have been these people.

As you read this book, I hope you'll learn that practicing good business etiquette doesn't mean being a suck-up or a pushover. It means treating yourself and others with respect and doing good work. It's an effort well spent, no matter what you do for a living.

PART ONE
THE BEST YOU

AT A PRESS CONFERENCE in Seoul, South Korea, in 2009, then–US Secretary of State Hillary Clinton observed that "showing up is not all of life, but it counts for a lot."

When it comes to business etiquette, showing up—and handling yourself well when you show up—is of paramount importance. Sure, you're brilliant and have the best ideas ever, but if you don't show up or if you're such a dolt when you show up that no one will listen to you, there will be scant opportunity for you to spread your brilliance around.

Practicing business etiquette doesn't mean pretending to be something you're not. It means being observant and respectful of others while remaining true to yourself.

For example, being prepared for a job interview doesn't mean you're not being yourself. It means you're making the most of your own and your interviewers' time by researching the company with which you're interviewing and getting ready to answer questions about your experience and how you see yourself fitting into a new business environment. Likewise, showing up to work on time is not a sign of weakness or sheep-like mentality. It's a sign that you respect the people with whom you work and recognize that their time is as important as your own. Dressing differently for work than you would for a Sunday game of cornhole at your buddy's house shows that you know the difference between work and play, and that you're observant enough to know what's acceptable attire in your workplace.

That ability to be observant and respectful while remaining true to yourself goes a long way toward laying a strong foundation of good business etiquette. This section of the book will help you learn how to be the best you—the one who helps set the norm for respectful behavior in your workplace, not the one who lets manners slip just because everyone else is doing it. It will show you how to be a cut above the rest—without being annoying about it.

"WAITER, THERE'S SOUP IN MY BEARD"

DRESS AND HYGIENE

I'm not going to hire you just because you're impeccably dressed and smell like a million bucks. But showing concern for how you look, smell, and generally take care of yourself does matter in most work settings. In other words, good dress and hygiene might not get you the job, but inappropriate dress and hygiene could lessen your chances of getting hired.

Appropriateness is key when it comes to considering how to dress for the job. On any job interview, cleanliness is a good rule of thumb for both your clothes and yourself. Of course, some workplaces are more formal than others, so once you're on the job, it helps to take cues from others about what's appropriate and what's not.

Early on in my career, when I was still in my twenties, I took a job with a small financial publisher located in the western suburbs of Boston. The location was dictated by the fact that the owner of the startup lived out there. He had had some success as a financial advisor and writer and was slowly building his company by adding a mostly young staff of writers and editors.

The boss's habit was to take each new hire out to lunch. He was an affable enough guy and the company was small enough that everyone knew one another, but that first lunch was often the first time many of us would have an extended private conversation with the boss. It could be nerve-racking.

When my time came, the boss called to let me know he was ready. I tossed on my sport jacket and walked downstairs to meet him at his office. We dressed as if we worked in an old, cheaply renovated barn, because we did. The only time I wore a tie was when I knew I'd be leaving the building to go out and interview someone for a story or attend an industry conference.

I had no idea what the boss would want to talk about at lunch, and I have no recollection of anything he said. But I do remember that when I asked him what he recommended, he told me that the New England clam chowder at this local restaurant was quite good. He ordered himself a bowl.

Back then, I sported a red beard and mustache. (Each has gone distinctly white since then.) I was conscious of the fact that the cream-based chowder, chock full of clams and potatoes and other gloppy stuff, might be challenging to navigate. I like clam chowder as much as the next Boston transplant, but I didn't want to risk looking like a slob by having soup particles attach themselves to my facial hair. Then again, the guy had just recommended this dish after I'd asked for his advice, and I didn't want to seem like I disregarded my boss's opinions.

How would you proceed?

A   Order a bowl of clam chowder and eat with abandon.

B   Order a small cup of clam chowder to reduce the volume of the possible beard mess.

C   Order a bowl but ask for an extra napkin just in case it becomes necessary to remove chowder from your beard.

D Order a bowl but make a joke about how hard it is to eat soup while sporting a full beard and mustache.

E Order the clam chowder, but pick at it gingerly and only take microscopic tastes.

F Order something else.

Choosing A suggests that you just don't care if you eat like a slob, whether in front of the boss or anyone. Having a hearty appetite may impress your nana, but it's unlikely to score points with anyone else. Option B doesn't help things at all if you plan to eat your cup of soup with as much abandon as you'd use to eat a full bowl. Asking for another napkin to dab away the vestiges of chowder left on your beard (C) means you know you'll be creating a sloppy appearance but you're going ahead with it anyway. And taking small spoonfuls (E) is only going to prolong the agony of worrying about soup while you try to talk with your boss. Ordering something else (F) would be a good option, although it'd be better if you hadn't asked for a recommendation in the first place.

What I actually did was D: I ordered the chowder but made what I thought was a witty comment about the challenge of not getting soup in my mustache. The boss—who also had a beard—replied, "That's why I trim mine."

In that one quick response, the boss made an indirect comment about my appearance that stuck. He didn't tell me that my beard was unkempt (although it probably was). He didn't tell me to go trim my beard (although he likely thought I should). He provided a practical response to a problem I joked about. In doing so, it became clear that appearance mattered to him—not enough to keep him from hiring me, but enough for him to offer advice when given the chance.

I didn't get rid of my beard and mustache, but I've since tried to keep them a bit more trimmed. It might not matter to me how they look, but it does send a message to others in the workplace about my grooming habits.

Granted, dealing with the length of a beard and mustache is an issue only for a subset of the population. But the lesson here is larger than a beard. That lesson is not that you should alter the way you present yourself in order to be something you're not—if you're looking to work at a place that requires you to change everything about the way you want to be, it's likely not the ideal place of employment for you. The lesson is that appearances do matter, and yours should be appropriate to the norms established wherever you work.

Take cues from colleagues about what's appropriate and what's not.

Here are some lessons I've learned when it comes to dress and hygiene in the workplace:

> Determine how formal your workplace is and dress accordingly.
> Always make sure that what you wear—formal or informal—is clean, unwrinkled, and appropriate.
> Be prepared to dress more formally on occasion.
> When in doubt about how formal a function is, ask someone. If he or she responds "business casual" and you haven't a clue what that means, ask. It's the kind of term whose definition can vary.
> Make sure to bathe regularly.
> Do not overuse cologne or perfume in the office. Strong scents can be distracting or cloying to others. Clean is good. Hyper-perfumed is not.
> Do not wear clothes that are too tight, too revealing, or that would cause discomfort to you or distraction to others in any other way.
> Trim your beard and mustache.

THE EARLY BIRD CATCHES THE WORK

PUNCTUALITY

B e on time. Whether it's to work or to a meeting, be on time. "Fashionably late" may cut it in some social circles, but not in a business setting. When you're late, it wastes others' time as well as your own. It is never good etiquette to be late.

A few years ago, Heathrow Express, a company that runs trains to and from Heathrow Airport in London, conducted a survey of British employees about lateness in the workplace. The survey, reported in the newspaper the *Independent* and elsewhere, found that 82 percent of those surveyed believed lateness was unprofessional. One-quarter of the survey participants believed arriving late to meetings adversely affected their own performance, while nearly half believed their lateness adversely affected others. It's not just during meetings that punctuality is often punctured. Ten percent of those surveyed acknowledged that they had been late to job interviews, and 11 percent acknowledged that lateness had cost them a prospective client.

The cost of employee lateness? In the United Kingdom alone, Heathrow Express estimated it to be £9 billion a year.

Based on the survey results, roughly 590,000 employees in the UK are late for work every day. Managers know lateness can be costly, and employees know that they're often late. Yet the problem persists—and obviously not just in the UK.

———

Recently, an employee, Jacob, asked his manager, Marisol, if she would take some time out of her schedule to meet with someone Jacob thought might be a good potential hire for the company. There were no openings at that time, but Marisol was always looking for good hires should jobs become available.

Now, Jacob had a reputation for being late to work, appointments, and meetings. His work was valuable, but it was a challenge to get him to show up on time. There was always a reason for the lateness—traffic, dropping off the kids at school, other meetings running late, a glitch in an online calendar, you name it.

Still, Marisol agreed to meet at a local coffee shop near the office where Jacob could introduce her to the prospect and the three of them could chat. Since Marisol didn't know the prospect, she was counting on Jacob to be there to make the introductions and get the conversation rolling.

The time for the meeting came. Marisol showed up on time, but she had no idea if the prospect was already in the coffee shop, because Jacob was nowhere to be found. Ten minutes passed. Still no Jacob.

Marisol had figured she would spend 30 minutes with the prospect and then return to her nearby office. But now she had already spent a good chunk of that time waiting . . . and she didn't know if the prospect was even in the coffee shop.

What would you do if you were Marisol?

Ⓐ Wait another five minutes and then leave.

Ⓑ Walk around the coffee shop and see if you can find the prospect.

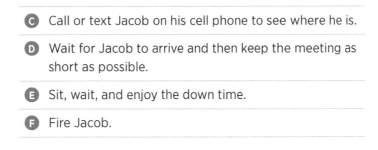

C Call or text Jacob on his cell phone to see where he is.

D Wait for Jacob to arrive and then keep the meeting as short as possible.

E Sit, wait, and enjoy the down time.

F Fire Jacob.

Marisol first tried C: calling her employee on his cell phone. When there was no answer, she texted him, letting him know that she had been waiting for 10 minutes for the meeting he had requested. No response.

After a couple more minutes, Marisol chose to do B. She looked around the coffee shop and saw someone sitting by himself. She approached him and asked if he was Jacob's former colleague. He was. Just as they sat down together to talk, Jacob breezed in.

"Oh, I'm glad you two found one another," he said, and then he sat and joined in the conversation. No apology. No acknowledgment of being late. No nothing.

The discussion among the three of them proved to be a bit forced, since the prospect seemed clearly uncomfortable about Marisol having to wait so long before Jacob arrived. Marisol was angry at Jacob for being late to a meeting he had set up, but she waited until they returned to the office to let him know.

The prospect was never considered for a job. While Jacob wasn't fired (F), he left within the year. It was clear that his challenge with punctuality did not mesh with the manager's expectations.

> It's rarely a problem to be early,
> and it's rarely okay to be late.

It's not just employees who are late to meetings. There are managers who regularly show up late to meetings without ever acknowledging the inconvenience or waste of time such behavior causes. When managers show up late, it sends a message that they don't care enough about their employees to value their time as much as they value their own.

Arguing that some business cultures find lateness acceptable is a dubious stance. It's like saying, "We just don't care about productivity or common courtesy." If being on time doesn't matter, then the meeting probably doesn't matter either. Save everyone time and only schedule events that are important enough for everyone to have to show up on time.

Here are some timely rules of thumb:

> Show up to work, meetings, and events on time, if not a bit early.

> If colleagues regularly show up late, remind them that you plan to start on time regardless of whether they're there.

> If you have a reputation for being late, then wake up earlier, leave the house earlier, leave your office earlier, and build in extra time to get to where you plan to be.

> It's rarely a problem to be a few minutes early to a meeting or appointment.

> It's rarely okay to be late.

> Make use of smartphone or online calendar alerts to help you plan ahead and get where you need to be on time.

> Stop reading this and get to where you need to be. The book will still be here when you're through.

DON'T STAND SO CLOSE TO ME

BODY LANGUAGE

The best way to use or interpret body language in the office is to be cognizant of it without overthinking it. You know what makes you comfortable or uncomfortable when it comes to how you stand, sit, look, speak, or smell in the workplace. Your own comfort levels, paired with a good dose of practicality, can be an effective guide to appropriate body language.

You don't need an expert to tell you just how many seconds of direct eye contact you can have with a coworker before you creep him out. But there are experts who can help you understand how your body language can make you or others comfortable or uncomfortable. In the early 1960s, cultural anthropologist Edward T. Hall developed a field of study he called "proxemics" to look at how we can use our personal space most effectively. You'll likely see Hall's work at play when you read guides or attend workshops discussing body language.

Hall broke down the optimal distance between people into four broad categories, each with a "close" and "far" phase:

> **intimate distance**
(close phase: less than 6 inches; far phase: 6 to 18 inches)
> **personal distance**
(close phase: 1.5 to 2.5 feet; far phase: 2.5 to 4 feet)
> **social distance**
(close phase: 4 to 7 feet; far phase: 7 to 12 feet)
> **public distance**
(close phase: 12 to 25 feet; far phase: 25 feet or more)

Some of Hall's work seems practical. If you're being intimate with someone, for example, it would be hard to plant a kiss while standing more than a foot and a half away. But then, kissing coworkers in the workplace is best kept to a minimum.

While Hall wasn't a slave to the exact measurements of these distances, he did create a whole science around how we touch, look, smell, and sound. He even studied the amount of body heat we give off. And if you want to know how intimate people in a conversation are, you could study Hall's "sociopetal–sociofugal axis," which has to do with the angle created by the shoulders of the people talking.

People will tell you this stuff matters. It might. But if you're overly self-conscious about distances or shoulder angles, you'll lose sight of the most important rule when it comes to body language in business: Don't go to ridiculous lengths to signal to others with your body what you could more easily do with specific words. (You certainly don't want to have to carry around a protractor to measure the angle between your shoulders and the shoulders of the guy in accounting when you're asking about payroll.) You know, after all, that if you want to shake someone's hand, you need to be close enough to her to reach her hand. If you happen to be able to shake hands when you're a bit farther than 4 feet apart, have at it. If you're addressing a crowd and the front row of listeners is closer than the optimal "public distance" of 12 feet, you know enough not to take out a tape measure and refuse to speak until the optimals are in place.

Ronaldo, a well-liked office colleague, had a problem—or rather, his coworkers had a problem with him. Whenever he engaged in conversation with a coworker, he sidled up very close and did a lot of touching. Consistent pats on the shoulders or arms. Lots of leaning in very close to talk even though his ability to project was not in question.

Coworkers backed away when the touching began, but Ronaldo didn't get the cue to back off. Again, they liked the guy. He was a great colleague and a nice fellow. But the touching and close-talking made them uncomfortable.

If you were one of Ronaldo's coworkers, what would you do to stave off the consistent invasion of your personal space?

A Report Ronaldo to a manager or human resources for inappropriate touching.

B Continue to back up or pull away whenever he touches you.

C Flee whenever you see him enter the room.

D Limit all contact with him to e-mail.

E Speak frankly but supportively to him about your discomfort with the touching, and ask him to stop.

F Mirror his behavior by speaking as loudly and closely as possible to him and start patting his shoulders and arms before he has a chance to go after yours.

None of Ronaldo's colleagues found the touching to be threatening or harassing (so no A), but they did find it annoying. Repeating the nonverbal body language of pulling back whenever he spoke or touched hadn't worked, so doing it over and over (B) was not assured to yield different results. Mirroring his behavior (F) might have backfired by suggesting to Ronaldo that it was perfectly okay to touch and talk as he did. Fleeing (C) or limiting contact to e-mail (D) would certainly have cut down on the physical interactions with

Ronaldo, but no one should have to hide physically or behind e-mail in the workplace.

The best solution, and the one that his colleagues implemented, was to speak frankly with Ronaldo (E). As each of them told him that the touching and close-talking made them a bit uncomfortable, Ronaldo tried to alter his behavior. It wasn't a perfect outcome, since he occasionally lapsed into old ways. But because his coworkers liked him and had an otherwise strong working relationship with him, his body language became more appropriate and less off-putting.

> Be cognizant of your body language,
> but don't overthink it.

Here's some basic etiquette when it comes to body language in the workplace:

> - Stand or sit up straight whenever possible. It not only sends a message of confidence and care, but it's also better for your spine.
> - Don't roll your eyes or make faces during meetings when you hear something you find to be ridiculous, unless it is agreed upon in your workplace that you will send signals to one another whenever one of you is talking nonsense.
> - Allow enough space between you and the person you're speaking with to avoid any discomfort. If you're a rule-of-thumb type and need a number, figure on leaving a space of at least half of your height.
> - When you're speaking one-on-one, look directly at the other person's face. You needn't gaze into his or her eyes if you don't want to—instead you can look at the person's mouth. A side benefit of this tactic is that if you're talking with a soft-spoken person, you can also read their lips as they speak for better comprehension.

- Avoid crossing your arms tightly in front of your body when you're speaking. It gives the impression that you are either tense or incredibly cold. (If you're the latter, get a sweater.)
- Feel free to use hand gestures when you're speaking if that's something that feels natural to you. Avoid using them solely because someone told you to, if doing so makes you feel self-conscious.
- Most often, trust your instincts. If you're uncomfortable with your own body language, try something else. If you're uncomfortable with someone else's, try to find a way to change how you interact with that person.
- Don't overthink your or others' body language. Sometimes people stand or speak or look at you the way they do because that's just the way they stand or speak or look at everyone.
- Don't gawk at others during meetings or at any other time. It's creepy.

PLEASED TO MEET YOU (HOPE YOU GUESSED MY NAME)

INTRODUCTIONS

Everything I know about the proper way to introduce people to one another I learned from my mother-in-law, Cae.

Growing up, I had learned decent table manners (no elbows on the table) and how to answer a telephone courteously enough ("Hello, may I ask who's calling?"), but I was oblivious to the fact that there was a protocol for introducing one person to the next. Perhaps this was due to the fact that by the time I was ready to learn, my grandparents were long gone, and I had no memory of them.

But Cae had nine grandchildren, two of whom were my children. Often the grandkids would visit her with friends, and when they did, she taught them that the proper way to introduce their friends was to say, "Nana, this is my friend Theresa." Unless, of course, the friend's name wasn't Theresa—but you get the idea. Out of respect for her status as grandmother, the right thing to do was to introduce the friend to her, rather than introducing her to the friend.

The same went for us as her kids or kids-in-law. When we introduced someone to Cae, it was, "Cae, this is my friend Theresa" (lots of Theresas in my neighborhood), not the other way around. It took me a while to get the order straight. I had a 50-50 shot and, at first, often remembered the rule backward. But Cae kindly corrected me, and it stuck.

This basic rule of introductions follows through to the workplace. When you're introducing people in the workplace, you generally introduce the lower-ranking person to the higher-ranking person. I know that many blanch at the idea of hierarchies in the workplace, but they still exist. Being consistent with how you introduce people also takes away the possibility of getting flummoxed over how to do it when the need arises.

So if a colleague from another department visits your department, you'd introduce that colleague to your boss (if she didn't know her already) by saying, "Boss, this is Theresa." If someone from outside the company visits (a friend, family member, or worker from another company, perhaps), you'd follow the same protocol: "Boss, this is my sister, Theresa."

Now, that's all fine and good, and you're likely to remember the rule more quickly than I did. But sometimes a challenge arises where you're put in the position of having to introduce someone whose name you've forgotten.

Every spring, a department of a larger company chartered a boat to take its employees out for a two-hour cruise up and down a river. Food and drink were provided. Some former employees and some from other departments were also invited. Since there was little possibility for escape once the boat was launched onto the river, the likelihood of running into most of the other passengers at some point during that captive two hours was great.

Leigh was never a fan of the boat cruise, not because he didn't like his fellow employees, but because he felt stuck. He couldn't leave early if he wanted to, unless he chose to jump overboard and swim to shore, something he was pretty sure was frowned upon by both his management and the boat's operators. At other land-based company outings, Leigh could always cut out early after he had spent some quality time with colleagues. But not on the boat.

Still, Leigh more often than not joined his colleagues on the boat cruise, because it was a good chance to relax with coworkers, and the food and drink weren't bad either.

As the boat pulled away from shore one spring, Leigh began to walk around the top deck. He and Rick, a coworker, soon started talking. Within minutes, Leigh saw a woman he recognized walking toward him. She had worked in his department years ago but had transferred to another department in a different city shortly after he started.

"Hi, Leigh!" she called out.

Leigh couldn't for the life of him remember her name, so he was at a loss about how he was going to introduce Rick to her.

What would you do?

A Avoid the issue and just start talking.

B Feign ignorance and pretend you've never met her.

C Ask her to remind you of her name.

D Tell Rick you have to hit the head and flee before she gets to you.

E Start the conversation by saying something to the effect of "How are you? This is my colleague, Rick."

F Call her Theresa and hope for the best.

Given that Leigh had made eye contact with the former colleague, fleeing (D) was not appropriate. Flee to where? He was on a boat. Feigning ignorance (B) when he truly remembered her would be not only rude but also dishonest. Guessing her name and potentially calling her by the wrong name (F) would be worse than not saying a name at all.

He didn't know the former colleague well (she'd transferred during his first few weeks on the job), so it would be reasonable to comment about how he knew her and to ask her to remind him of her name (C). But he didn't feel comfortable acknowledging right out that he didn't remember her name, especially because she had called him by name. Just starting the conversation and not bringing up names (A) would remove the possibility that he'd get her name wrong, but then he might never learn what she was actually called.

Choosing E, Leigh introduced the former colleague to Rick. Like many people, she followed suit by saying, "It's good to meet you, Rick. My name is Theresa."

If you find yourself being introduced to someone in this way, make sure to do as Theresa did and introduce yourself by name to Rick. Doing so diffuses what could otherwise be an awkward situation.

Introduce yourself by name.

If you know you're going to introduce someone, here are some general guidelines:

> Make sure you know how that person prefers to be introduced. Even if she uses a nickname at work, she might prefer that others learn her given name on first introduction.

> Introduce the lower-ranking person to the higher-ranking person. ("Nancy, this is Lucas, who works in shipping.")

> Introduce those from outside the company to those from inside the company. ("Outside guy, this is inside guy." Or, "Bob, this is my boss Fred. Fred, this is Bob, our customer from Boise.")

> Introduce customers to employees.

> Do not guess at someone's name if you don't remember it.

> Always introduce others to your grandmother, even if they "technically" outrank her.

And here are some general guidelines if you know you're going to be introduced:

> Let the person who will introduce you know if you prefer to be introduced by a certain name.

> If someone introduces someone else by name, follow suit by telling that person your name.

> If someone gets your name wrong, correct it by telling the person, "You can call me Theresa." But only if your name is Theresa.

LET'S TALK ABOUT ME. WHAT DO YOU THINK ABOUT ME?

BEING INTERVIEWED

Aoife was on a job interview. She was a finalist for a position that looked pretty plum, and the company had flown her to its site so key managers and employees could interview her in person. Aoife really wanted to make a good impression. She also wanted to get a good sense of whether, should the job be offered, it was worth relocating, since a move would require her spouse to relocate, too, or the couple to live in separate cities throughout the workweek.

She spent time preparing for the job interviews, studying as much as she could about the company and the people she'd been told would interview her. She also put significant time into preparing a short presentation to give to several employees and managers at the company.

She arrived the night before her first meetings and checked into the hotel where the company had arranged for her to stay. The interviews began the next morning over breakfast in the hotel restaurant with two of the company's managers.

All went well throughout the morning. She was asked questions about her prior work and how she saw it fitting in with this prospective new position. She was not asked any questions that seemed off-limits (e.g., anything about health, family, religion, political views). Aoife asked each team of interviewers questions about the company, their jobs, and their work environment and began to get a feel for the people and the place.

The interviews continued over lunch, and Aoife still felt that the questioners seemed genuinely interested in her, her skills, and what she might bring to the company.

After lunch, however, she was to meet with Jack, a senior manager who ran the division and who she was pretty sure would have a strong say in who ultimately got the job. Several people had given her a heads-up that the fellow could be a bit prickly. "Don't let his gruffness bother you," one employee had told her during the morning interview. "It's just how he is."

When Aoife entered Jack's office suite, his assistant asked her to have a seat, since Jack was running a bit late. A good 15 minutes passed before Jack asked his assistant to send Aoife into his office. When she entered the room, Jack stood up to shake her hand but didn't come out from behind his desk. They each sat, and what appeared to be the formal interview began.

"You seem to have a pretty good job," Jack said. "Why would you want to uproot yourself and come work here?"

Aoife told Jack about her desire to try new challenges, what she perceived to be the strengths of Jack's company, and how she believed she might be able to contribute based on her skills.

Jack then picked up Aoife's résumé, took a close look at it, and said, "Your résumé is confusing."

"How so?" asked Aoife.

Jack told Aoife that he found it difficult to follow where she worked because she had listed her full-time work chronologically in one place and her independent consulting clients chronologically in another place.

No one else who'd interviewed her had seemed to have a problem following the course of her career as represented on her résumé. It had clearly been strong enough to make her a finalist for this position. But Jack kept pushing at what he found to be the confusing nature of her résumé. "Why wouldn't you put everything together in one place to avoid confusion? Is there something you're trying to hide by setting up the résumé this way? Have other prospective employers understood where you worked and when?"

"Take this as constructive feedback," Jack told Aoife. "You're going to want to clean this résumé up to make it more understandable as you move along."

Aoife was silent, calculating what the best response to Jack's "confusion" might be. She felt insulted, but she was still on a job interview, and Jack was a clear decision-maker about new hires. Still, she couldn't help but feel that Jack was a bit aggressive about the setup of Aoife's résumé, enough so that it was pretty much all they'd talked about up to that point.

How would you respond to Jack?

A Tell Jack that no one else seemed to have trouble understanding the résumé, so perhaps he should get one of his colleagues to walk him through the document.

B Try to redirect the conversation back to the open position and how you might fit in at the company.

C Patiently explain to Jack why you set up your résumé the way you did, and then segue into a discussion of how your past experience is relevant for the new job.

D Ask Jack to show you his résumé so you can have a sense of what brilliance looks like.

E Tell Jack that his focus on résumé structure rather than your potential fit for the job seems inappropriate.

F Stand up while Jack is still talking, thank him for his time, and walk out of his office, never to return.

While Aoife's interaction with Jack might have given her pause about whether this was a company for which she wanted to work, she still needed to keep her options open should she be offered the position. So she wanted to make the conversation with Jack as civil as possible. Telling him that he should have all her other interviewers explain her résumé to him (A) would be intended as a slight and probably wouldn't help her get a job offer. Similarly, asking Jack to show her his résumé if he was so good at them (D) would at best be meant as a challenge and at worst as an insult. Neither would have advanced Aoife's case as a strong prospective hire. The same goes for standing up and walking out (F).

While telling Jack that it was inappropriate to focus on résumé structure rather than Aoife's qualifications (D) might have redirected the interview, choices B and C are more positive attempts to achieve the same result. While B would have avoided an explanation for Jack's résumé concern, it would have allowed Aoife to try to get the discussion focused on her and what she brings to the table.

The route she took, however, was C. By responding to Jack's observations about her résumé with an explanation and then moving on to a broader discussion of herself and the prospective job, Aoife did not appear dismissive of Jack's structural obsession, but she still showed her ability to accomplish the primary goal of their interview meeting. Jack still didn't like the way she set up her résumé, but at least he knew she was listening to him.

Showcase the strengths
you'll bring to the position.

Here are some things to keep in mind when you're being interviewed for a position:

> Always try to keep the discussion on you, your strengths, and how those strengths might fit with the new company.
> Prepare yourself by doing research on the company and any key employees who might be scheduled to interview you.

> Know that you'll likely be one of many candidates who are asked the same questions. Even when stock questions are asked, work to make your answers stand out by being very specific and showing that you have an understanding of the company and the open job.

> If you have gaps in your résumé, be prepared with an explanation.

> Be prepared to answer why you're leaving your current job. Avoid bad-mouthing your current or former company.

> Don't offer any more information than is essential to the questions asked. Going off on long tangents about your days as a spelunker is not likely to help you, unless you're directly asked about your days as a spelunker or you're applying for a job as a spelunker.

> If you're being interviewed by phone, one old trick is to resist the urge to fill every silence between questions. Answer the questions asked and then wait for the next one. Silences are uncomfortable, and the temptation is to fill them. ("Did I tell you I'm a spelunker?") Avoid the temptation. Let the interviewer fill any silences once you have answered the question.

> If you're being interviewed by a group of people, don't direct all your answers to just one person. Try to engage all the interviewers in the group in the discussion.

> If one of the people who interviews you turns out to be a bit of a jerk, don't feel compelled to tell him he's a jerk. Use the experience as one of many cues to help you decide whether this is a place you'd want to work should you be offered the job.

ASK A BOSS

WHAT'S THE BEST OR WORST IMPRESSION THAT A CANDIDATE HAS MADE ON YOU?

Ann Handley, chief content officer of MarketingProfs and author of *Everybody Writes: Your Go-To Guide to Creating Ridiculously Good Content* and *Content Rules: How to Create Killer Blogs, Podcasts, Videos, Ebooks, Webinars (and More) That Engage Customers and Ignite Your Business*, tells me that her best hire was a virtual one. The prospective employee had Skype on her work computer, but she didn't want her boss to know she was looking for a new job. "So she downloaded Skype to her smartphone, drove to a Dunkin' Donuts parking lot near her office, and Skyped me at the appointed hour from there," writes Handley. "The quality was terrible and she had a hard time figuring out how to best use it on her phone (sun glare, etc.), but she persisted and never lost her poise or her cool. It was a 'make it work' moment, and that told me a lot about how she'd handle the frequent stress around here. It also told me that she'd do whatever she could to get the job done, because she owned it and made it happen versus coming up with excuses!"

Mike Hofman, executive digital director at *GQ*, was once turned off by a guy who was "somewhat qualified" for a creative position but made a terrible first impression "by being late, sweaty, and making it clear his true passion was acting."

For Dean Miller, a senior vice president of content at Connecticut Public Broadcasting, typos in a résumé or cover letter are a killer. But his worst, he writes, was a parent "showing up at the workplace with the entry-level employee, day one."

PART TWO

OFFICE CULTURE

THE WORD *CULTURE* has a few meanings. In business, it refers to the established norms of behavior in a workplace. In biology, it refers to the cultivation of bacteria in an artificial medium. Perhaps the definitions aren't that far apart if you think of your workplace as a petri dish where you and your coworkers are cultivated to do good work together.

Before it was common for infants and toddlers to spend their days in child care while their parents worked, children were often in for a shock when they were sent off to kindergarten and had to learn for the first time to share and play well with others. When we enter into a workplace, we, too, have to learn to work and play with our colleagues in unselfish ways.

"Wait," you're saying. "Did he just call me a child? Did he just call me a germ?" I have too much respect for you to think of you as a germ or a child. You are a full-grown, able, intelligent, hardworking, respectful adult.

But if you want to succeed in business, you do have to learn to work and play well with others in your workplace. You need to be observant of your workplace's culture—what's deemed appropriate and what's not. Again, you should never try to be something you're not. But you should try to be your best you in a way that is respectful of your colleagues.

When I had to give a talk to all the incoming freshmen at a college where I used to teach, I asked my grandson Evan, who was just starting kindergarten, what he was most worried about on his first day of school. He thought for a moment, then answered, "Making friends. And not falling down."

If you're observant about and respectful of your office culture, you're more likely to form collegial and productive work relationships without falling down on the job. This section of the book will help you learn how to do just that.

SMALL TALK IS A BIG DEAL

MAKING SMALL TALK

In a 2015 survey conducted by Accountemps, gossiping about coworkers was deemed to be the worst etiquette faux pas in the workplace. Twenty-eight percent of workers surveyed put gossip at the top of their list of "biggest etiquette offenses." Yet it remains a problem, because people continue to do it.

The most practical solution when faced with an office gossiper is to disengage from the discussion or change the subject as quickly as possible. There's no valor in allowing yourself to engage in a bit of pettiness or outright character assassination just to humor the gossipmonger. Don't engage in gossip if you don't want to give it a place in your office.

A healthy office culture offers little room for gossiping about coworkers. But healthy office cultures—and most dysfunctional ones as well—do require us to talk with one another regularly. When the talk is about a work project, the discussion can flow well enough, since the point of departure for the discussion is clear. It's small talk and casual conversations that can trip many people up. Some colleagues are naturally poised and extroverted and seem to have little trouble engaging others in conversation. But there are just as many who find making small talk awkward or anxiety-producing.

"What if I say something wrong?"

"What if I sound like an idiot?"

"How do I respond if a coworker inadvertently insults me?"

"Why do these people keep talking to me?"

All fair questions, but when we enter a workplace, it's fair to assume we're going to have to talk with others working there.

At a relatively large organization with more than 11,000 employees, it's possible to run across coworkers you've never met before or have met only occasionally. Harry worked at such an organization. His job was in public affairs, where he wrote press releases and speeches for the company's executives and coached employees on how to speak to the media when they were representing the company.

Nina ran another division of the company. She and Harry rarely, if ever, came in contact with one another, since they worked in different buildings across town from each other. But over the years, Nina had often contacted Harry with a request that he come to her office to do special trainings for her top managers who regularly talked to the media. While doing so fell outside Harry's specific job description, he routinely agreed to take on the task. Nina's employees seemed to enjoy his instruction and find it useful.

Several times a year, Harry's office and Nina's division were invited to events together. Harry figured they'd both been to at least a half dozen of these events over the past three years. On each occasion, a mutual colleague who regularly worked with both Nina and Harry took the time to make sure Harry and Nina had been introduced. It was never the same mutual colleague who tried to make the introduction. Everyone was wearing name tags with their names and functions on them.

On each occasion, the interaction had gone like this: "Nina, have you met Harry from our public affairs office?" (Nina outranked Harry in the company hierarchy, so the mutual colleague seems to have learned good business etiquette when it comes to introductions.)

Each time, Nina responded, "I don't believe we have," and extended her hand to shake Harry's hand.

Now, the first time this happened, Harry was taken aback. Surely, Nina knew his name—she regularly called on him for the favor of training her employees. Even though she wasn't at the trainings herself, Nina was the one who had sent the e-mails to Harry making the requests. On that first occasion, Harry figured maybe his name didn't register with her. But when the same thing happened at the next event where they were introduced, it began to strike Harry as thoughtless if not rude behavior.

How would you respond to Nina's claim of ignorance about your being?

A Shake Nina's hand and act as if you indeed never had met.

B Politely remind Nina that you had met before as a result of the trainings you regularly conducted for her workers.

C Whenever you notice Nina from a distance at an event, do everything in your power to avoid getting near her.

D Tell Nina that if she keeps failing to remember who you are, you'll never take the time to conduct another training for her employees.

E Don a porkpie hat, look Nina directly in the eyes, and say, "Say my name."

While avoiding Nina (C) was tempting, it would have done little to correct the situation. Avoiding small talk, no matter how uncomfortable, is rarely a practical approach. Harry did nothing wrong, so aside from perhaps feeling unappreciated or unnoticed, he had no reason to have to hide from . . . what's her name? . . . oh right, Nina. Harry could have feigned ignorance of who Nina was (A), but while that might have avoided the immediate awkwardness, it wouldn't address the situation at hand. Option D might have been tempting since Harry felt slighted by Nina's lack of recognition, but a social event was not the right time to lash out. Harry could decide later if he wanted to continue doing Nina a favor by running trainings for her employees. And unless he chose to start going by the name "Heisenberg," E is a silly response—plus few of us can pull off the porkpie-hat look well.

Harry's response was to remind Nina that they'd met and in what context (B), and then move on with the small talk. Nina was a bit embarrassed, but Harry quickly proceeded to another topic of discussion, one related to the work he'd done with her employees. By taking this approach, Harry showed grace and forthright-ness. He followed a good rule of thumb: Rarely is it appropriate to respond to apparent rudeness with your own rudeness.

Harry's ability to engage in small talk when faced with a col-league who he thought was being rude showed true grit. Instead of letting his ego get bruised, he eased the conversation by discuss-ing something positive about the work he had done for Nina's direct reports.

The key with small talk is to stay positive, keep the conversation focused on non-personal issues that relate to your mutual interests, and engage everyone in the conversation. Learning to use small talk well—and to distinguish it from office gossip—can save you from many dangerous situations.

Talk with your coworkers—not about them.

Here are some things to consider when making small talk in the office:

> Avoid gossiping about coworkers. If others bring it up, change the subject or walk away.

> Avoid asking overly personal questions about family, politics, religion, or other issues unless they directly have to do with work.

> Don't follow what might seem like an insensitive or rude comment by being insensitive or rude in response.

> When in doubt, ask about a coworker's work or their progress on a project.

> If you're talking with more than one person, make sure to engage everyone present in the conversation.

> Make an effort to listen and be responsive to what your coworker is saying.

> Never allow small talk to get in the way of doing your job. If you need to get back to work, politely excuse yourself and return to your desk.

COMMON SENSITIVITY

BEING SENSITIVE TOWARD OTHERS

There's a terrific passage in Tracy Kidder's book *Mountains Beyond Mountains*, which profiles infectious-disease specialist Dr. Paul Farmer and his work in Haiti. In the book, Kidder quotes Farmer: "I feel ambivalent about selling my services in a world where some can't buy them. You *can* feel ambivalent about that, because you *should* feel ambivalent. *Comma*."

This was one of many instances where Kidder heard Farmer use the word *comma* at the end of a sentence. He quickly learned that Farmer used the word *comma* as a stand-in for a specific word that would have followed an actual comma in his sentence, which was *asshole*. Many people apparently knew what he meant, and it was most often directed at "third parties" who "felt comfortable with the current distribution of money and medicine in the world." But by using the word *comma*, Farmer, whom Kidder described in his book as "almost invariably courteous," showed sensitivity to the fact that some people might find his use of the stronger term objectionable.

A comma is someone who doesn't show sensitivity to others. Don't be a comma. It's a good idea to be sensitive to others if you want people to want to work with you. That's not to say you have to carry it to the other extreme. Being overly sensitive about every possible offense anyone could take from anything you might say or do is unnecessary. Coworkers aren't fragile teacups who may crack at any moment. (If they are, it's their responsibility to deal with those issues outside of the workplace.)

Being sensitive means being aware that not everyone shares everyone else's comfort levels with particular language, actions, or manner. Mostly, sensitivity to others is just common sense. You already know that name-calling rarely shows sensitivity. Neither does suggesting a coworker is flawed because he doesn't complete a project as you might have or because she questions a procedure that you would sooner let go. By keeping focused on the work and not your coworkers' personalities, you'll avoid lapsing into insensitive behavior.

At an educational software startup that focused on creating interactive books, some employees had a great deal of editorial experience but scant coding experience, while others were great coders but didn't know how to edit. The owners of the company needed both skill sets to build the best product possible. The hope was that, gradually, staff members would adapt to one another's skills and abilities.

The editors would develop content and work with the founders and some of the coders to decide which parts of the books should be interactive. Using proprietary tools, the coders would then work to bring that interactive vision to life.

Some back-and-forth discussion between coders and editors would occur when coders needed clarification on what exactly the editors wanted users to be able to do with the interactive books. Sometimes coders would listen to the editors and offer an alternative they believed might reach the end goal more effectively.

As the individual interactive books drew closer to completion, the coders would present a build of the product that users could test to assess any flaws in the design. To get to this stage required making sure that the build actually worked and tweaking the coding if needed.

As one of these builds drew near, Robin, a coder, was working with Benny, an editor, to put the finishing touches on one of the interactive books. Benny had a distinct idea of how the book should work, but he didn't have the coding skills that Robin had to make it do what it needed to do. So the two of them went back and forth on some final details to get the book ready for the testing that was to begin the next day.

Benny pulled up a chair next to Robin's desk and began to ask questions about why the design so far didn't account for all the features the editorial team had requested.

"If we try to include all the features," Robin told Benny, "the product will never get done."

"But you've known the book was due for testing for weeks," Benny responded.

"You need to prioritize," Robin responded. She turned the screen so Benny could see it and began to explain all that was involved in changing the code.

Benny was lost. Editorial made sense to him. Coding, not so much. But Robin continued to talk. "I don't think you guys really have a clear idea of what you want," she said.

As Robin turned from the screen to look at Benny, it was clear that his eyes were welling up with tears. Robin sensed that Benny was overwhelmed, but she also knew that testing had to begin the next day.

If you were Robin, what action would you take?

A Keep explaining. The best way to address someone overwhelmed by code talk is to talk more code.

B Pause. Look at the screen. Look at Benny. Then say, "Are you crying? There's no crying in coding."

C Suggest taking a break and coming back to the discussion in a few minutes. ("Clear eyes. Full hearts. Can't lose.")

D Pat Benny on the shoulder and say, "Calm down. It's just a book."

E Wait a moment and ask Benny how the two of you might work together to get the project done in time for tomorrow's testing.

With apologies to all my coder friends, talking more code to those who don't get it (A) shows insensitivity. When working with those whose expertise is different from your own, remember that just because you find something easy to comprehend does not mean everyone does. Unless Robin and Benny were good friends and enjoyed a good laugh, option B was likely to insult Benny and make things worse. If they were friends and knew the other was willing to laugh at him- or herself under stressful conditions, then adding a bit of levity to lessen the tension wouldn't be a bad idea. Be sensitive to what you know about the person you're working with before trying to lighten the mood. Patting of any sort (D) usually accompanies condescension. Condescension is not sensitivity. Condescension is demeaning. Condescension would not get Robin and Benny's interactive book ready in time for testing.

Robin decided to step back and suggest a break (C). After the break, she redirected the conversation to ways in which she and Benny could work together to get things done (E). Both these actions showed sensitivity to the situation and to her coworker's clear distress in the moment.

Listen and engage.

You shouldn't have to walk on tiptoes around coworkers. But you should show sensitivity to them if you hope to have a productive work relationship. To do so, keep these things in mind:

> Try to listen to coworkers and assess their comfort levels with your demeanor.
> Avoid offensive language or other vulgarities that might make a coworker uncomfortable.
> Listen to your coworkers without cutting them off midsentence.
> Engage all coworkers in the discussion about a project for which their input is needed.
> Don't be abrupt or condescending.
> Be cognizant that coworkers with different fields of expertise might not easily understand your field of expertise.
> Don't be a comma.

E-MAIL CHAIN OF FOOLS

WRITING AND
SENDING E-MAILS

S ara Radicati, a technology market researcher in Palo Alto,
California, puts the number of e-mails sent and received a day
at more than 108.7 billion. Among these billions of messages, 1,425
now sit in my main inbox, 101 of them unread. I'm between semes-
ters as I write this, so my volume of daily e-mail is decidedly lower
than usual. So far today, I've received 94 e-mails. And the day
is young.

In another three years, Radicati estimates that more than
139.4 billion e-mails will be flung daily. Your goal? Stop the madness.
Or at the very least, control the number of e-mails you write and
what you write in them. If you really don't need to send an e-mail,
don't send it. If you want the person sitting in the cubicle next to you
to tell you what happened in the staff meeting you missed, walk next
door and ask him. (Better still, show up to the staff meeting.)

What you do on your own time with your own e-mail account
is your business. But keep in mind that 43 percent of companies
monitor their employees' e-mail, and so far, the law is on their side.
Many of the companies that track e-mail do it automatically with

technology, but a good 40 percent of those who monitor e-mails assign an actual person to read your messages and make sure you aren't up to anything hinky.

What happens when things get hinky in your e-mail? Hell can rain down.

Several years ago, an employee at a large brokerage firm in St. Louis started receiving e-mails that contained "inappropriate" material. You know, off-color jokes, pornography, that sort of thing. Not the sort of stuff that might land you in jail, but offensive nonetheless. The company had a zero-tolerance policy about sending inappropriate e-mail. A principal at the company told me at the time that all the employees knew about the policy, but apparently that didn't keep everyone from hitting the send button.

Now, many of us receive the occasional e-mail we might find inappropriate, offensive, or a waste of time. When the e-mails come from someone outside the company, you can delete them, ask the sender not to forward them, or even set up a block to keep any of his or her messages from hitting your inbox.

But what if you receive an inappropriate e-mail at work from a colleague? How should you respond?

A Delete.

B Delete and ask the sender never to darken your inbox with such nonsense again.

C Forward the e-mail on to others in the company who might enjoy a good laugh at offensive material.

D Add a few offensive quips of your own and send them along.

E Report the culprit to the human resources department.

F Ignore and get on with life at work.

At this St. Louis brokerage firm, quite a few of the roughly 2,700 employees with e-mail access apparently chose options C and D. Most of the rest chose F, which in itself did nothing to stem the tide of rampant e-mail excess. Finally, the employee mentioned earlier filed a complaint with the HR department (E), and an investigation was launched.

It turns out that it wasn't just one fellow who was sending around errant e-mails. And it's certain that the employee who went to HR wasn't the first to receive one. When the dust settled, depending on what the principal told me was "the egregiousness of their involvement," 19 employees were dismissed, 1 was permitted to resign, and 41 received warnings about their behavior.

The takeaway I offered readers when I reported this story was simple: "Don't do anything you wouldn't want to be caught doing."

Don't send anything you wouldn't
want to be caught sending.

Here are some larger lessons when it comes to writing and sending e-mails:

> Don't e-mail jokes on company e-mail.
> Don't assume you know what colleagues will find offensive in e-mail.
> If you have a personal e-mail to send to a colleague, send it from your personal e-mail account to theirs.
> If a colleague sends you an inappropriate e-mail, don't forward it along to other colleagues.
> Don't send offensive material to colleagues, even if you do it on your own time and via your own e-mail.
> If you would be embarrassed if an e-mail were to be read by others, don't send it.

When you do send an e-mail, here are some good basic rules of e-mail etiquette:

> Keep your work e-mails short, to the point, and related to work.
> Whenever you can simply say something to a colleague directly rather than commit it to an e-mail, do it.
> Don't use the "high importance" e-mail function on each e-mail you send. No one's e-mails are all that important.
> Avoid using the mechanism that requires recipients to indicate they've received your e-mail. That's just annoying, and most recipients will avoid it anyway.
> Proofread your e-mails for typos and grammatical errors.
> Think about typing your e-mail message first before putting the name of the recipient in the "To" field. This will save you from inadvertently sending an e-mail that is half written or that you haven't had time to fully consider.
> Make sure not to hit "Reply All" on e-mails when you really want to respond just to the sender.
> Don't be the jerk who sends annoying e-mails around the office.

GAME OF PHONES

SPEAKING
ON THE PHONE

My landline phone at work mostly sits idle. If someone needs to reach me, they generally do so by sending an e-mail. My voice-mail on the office phone lets a caller know that if he or she needs to reach me right away, they should consider e-mailing me. I'm likely to see an e-mail on my smartphone long before I retrieve a voice-mail on my landline phone.

If a longer conversation is needed, I do talk by phone or occasionally via Skype, but the instances of my landline phone ringing have grown infrequent.

Still, there are some basic rules of etiquette you'll need when it comes to making or receiving business phone calls, whether on a landline or a cell phone.

One of these rules is to try to keep the phone call as civil as possible.

For the weekly ethics column I write, I regularly call experts for information on a particular topic about which I'm writing.

Several years ago, I was writing about employee stock-ownership plans (ESOPs). I had often heard that companies using ESOPs outperformed those that did not, but I was never able to find research that supported this claim. On the advice of a former colleague, I contacted "Adam," who I was told had research on this topic that might be helpful.

Over e-mail, we set up a time for a call. When I called him, he answered with good phone etiquette, introducing himself by name ("This is Adam"). I introduced myself according to good phone etiquette as well: "Hello, this is Jeffrey Seglin. I write a weekly column on ethics and had e-mailed you about your ESOPs research." We were off to a great start.

Adam was quite enthusiastic about ESOPs. When I asked if he could point me to any research showing that companies using ESOPs outperformed those that didn't, he enthusiastically told me that it was intuitive to believe this was the case and enthusiastically explained why.

I agreed that, intuitively, it may indeed make sense that employees rewarded with company stock might perform better, which might translate into a better-performing company. But did he have any research that proved this to be true?

Adam told me that his own research showed that ESOP companies clearly outperformed non-ESOP companies. No question.

At this point, the telephone conversation was still proceeding civilly. I had called him for information, and he had been kind enough to take the time to respond to my questions.

But then I asked him for specifics: By what percentage do these ESOP companies outperform non-ESOP companies?

Adam seemed taken aback. He enthusiastically told me I was questioning his credibility by asking him to substantiate his claims and enthusiastically ended his response with a two-word expletive.

I reminded him that I was simply seeking information for a column.

He repeated the expletive—although, granted, he didn't raise his voice, which I must admit is good practice when talking on the phone.

It seemed he either didn't have the information or wasn't willing to share it with me.

I thanked him for talking to me, but before we hung up, he told me that he'd purchased a table at an upcoming industry association dinner in my city and asked if I'd like to join him and his colleagues for dinner.

Typically, I don't let sources for stories pay for my dinner. And I'm not a huge fan of industry dinners of any sort, though I politely attend from time to time. But I was at a bit of a loss as to how to respond, particularly after his repetition of some choice words in response to my earlier questions.

How would you appropriately respond to Adam during this phone call?

A Thank him for the invitation, but decline.

B Remind him that he's just been rude on the phone so you're baffled about why he would make such an invitation.

C Hang up.

D Tell him you'll go to dinner if he'll either share his research with you or acknowledge he doesn't have any such research.

E Repeat his expletive back at him.

Hanging up (C) or returning his inappropriate words to him (E) might have given me a momentary sense of having the upper hand, but neither would achieve much in the long term. If we start behaving badly in response to everyone who behaves badly toward us, we're doomed to be a society of miscreants. Reminding Adam he'd just been rude (B) wouldn't achieve much either. He knew what he said. I knew what he said. Option D, using an acceptance to his dinner invitation as leverage to get a clearer answer from him, was more likely to yield another two-word epithet than the response I wanted.

Thanking him but declining (A) was the appropriate way to go and the way I did respond. He seemed disappointed, but then the world is full of quirky people.

Throughout my conversation with Adam, it was important to keep the tone as civil and on-topic as I could, even when he was doing the opposite. It's not just good phone behavior to keep calls under control and to the point—it also saves you from wasting time on the phone when you could be doing more productive work.

Speak clearly.

In addition to introducing yourself, clearly stating your reason for calling, being civil, and staying on point, here are some things to keep in mind when placing or answering a phone call:

> Avoid using speakerphone when possible. If you are using speakerphone, make sure to inform the person on the other end of the call.

> If you're using a headset, make sure the person on the other end can hear you.

> Speak clearly.

> Try to avoid interrupting the other caller. Doing so is not only rude—it also makes it difficult for both parties to hear what each other is saying.

> Thank the person for the call and/or the information received on the call. If you believe you'll need to call again, ask the caller if and when that might be possible.

> Avoid hurling curse words at the caller, even if you find him or her annoying.

BREAKING OUT OF YOUR CELL

USING YOUR CELL
PHONE AT WORK

A t the college where I used to teach, I was part of a panel on the
ethics of publishing illustrations of Mohammed. The editors of
the school's newspaper had published one of the images, and there
was some reaction to that decision. It wasn't as much of an outcry
as might have been expected, but nevertheless, the president of
the college thought it was important for the school to have an open
discussion, as did the college chapter of the Society of Professional
Journalists, which I recall sponsored the panel.

The panel consisted of me, an imam from the local mosque, the
director of spiritual life at the college, the student president of the
college's Islamic Community, the newspaper's editor, and a handful
of others. More than 100 people showed up for the forum, including the college's president, who had expressed concern about the
civility members of the community showed one another. Each of
the panelists was asked to speak briefly, and then the floor would be
open to questions and comments from the audience.

When it came time for me to speak, a distinct sound filled the
theater: a cell phone's ringtone. It was difficult to determine where

the sound came from in the audience, but it kept ringing and ringing and ringing. Finally, the president of the college, who was sitting in the front row, put down her iPad, grabbed her bag, and searched around for her phone so she could silence it.

A bit of laughter and a round of applause followed when she shut the thing down. Had the phone been a student's, I'm not sure the level of tolerance for the disruption would have been so great.

We all make mistakes when it comes to managing our cell phones, mostly forgetting to turn them off when we're in a public setting where they can cause a major disruption. But we should all still make an effort to manage cell phones in a business setting, both to avoid disruption and to limit the amount of time spent on personal texts and social media when there's work to be done.

At a luncheon honoring several people who had fought for First Amendment rights, employees and affiliates of local businesses and organizations congregated around large tables. There were several awards, preceded by short introductions of the recipients. A host for the luncheon also gave a talk on the work that the awarding organization had done over the past year.

As the awards proceeded, several people in the room could be seen checking their cell phones for whatever it is people check their cell phones for when they're at a luncheon to honor something else. Phones didn't ring, but thumbs and fingers were working the screens.

At one point, Al, who was invited to sit at a table with others affiliated with his organization, noticed that the person next to him had his phone out and was typing away. He looked at the next seat and saw another fellow working his cell phone. The third seat down? Another guest thumbed away. And the guest in the fourth seat. And the fifth. Five people at a table of ten were typing away on their cell phones as people were being honored on the dais in the front of the room. Al noticed a smattering of people at other tables who were also paying attention to their cell phones rather than to the honorees.

Granted, some of these folks might have been tweeting about the comments being made up front. Live-tweeting can be an effective way to promote a cause. But none of the five at Al's table were on Twitter. They appeared to be e-mailing, text messaging, or otherwise engaged. (A later online check confirmed that very few tweets had gone out from the event.)

Al found it distracting to have to look over the thumbing colleagues toward the front of the room. What would you do in his place?

A Take a photo of the five of them on their phones and tweet it to the world.

B Stand up and loudly exclaim, "Would you get off your phones so we can pay attention to the people being honored?"

C Wait until after the event and then speak to each of the colleagues to let them know how disrespectful they had been.

D Post an embarrassing video of them to Vine.

E Discreetly ask the closest phone-thumber if he might hold off for a while, since his actions are distracting.

As tempting as options A and D might have been, they would have done little to resolve the issue at hand. Exclaiming loudly (B) would only further detract from those being honored and exhibit equally rude behavior. Some version of option C might have discouraged this behavior at future events, depending on Al's relationship with each of the five thumbers, but it would not have addressed the challenge of the moment: getting the guests to stop using their cell phones and start paying attention to the honorees.

Al quietly asked the colleague nearest him if he might stop texting for a bit, since he found it to be distracting (E). The colleague said, "Oh, sure, of course," and then asked the others if they could stop as well. They all did.

*Don't use your phone or let it ring
while someone else is talking.*

Most of us know it's rude to be on our phones while we're supposed to be doing something else. But there's a strange, insatiable draw to be connected all the time. Fight the urge. Savor the moment of cell-free life whenever you can. And don't be a rude thumber.

If your company has a policy against using personal cell phones during company time, then don't use your cell phone during company time. But more and more, employees use their cell phones for both personal and business use. If you're one of the latter, then consider the following tips:

> Turn the ringer off and set the phone to vibrate when you arrive at the office. That way you won't forget to turn the phone off during meetings or at other times when it would be rude to have it ring.

> If your business and personal lives aren't totally enmeshed, limit your personal calls and texts to your personal time.

> If you have an important call or text to make when you're at a social function, leave the room and make it from a corridor or someplace where you won't draw attention away from the event.

> If you're attending a meeting and are expecting a critical call that simply cannot wait, then inform your coworkers that you might have to leave for the call. Such instances should be rare. Few calls are that important.

> Avoid using your cell phone during business meals.

> If tweeting during a meeting or conference is encouraged, then limit your cell phone use to tweeting. Don't pretend to tweet about the event when you're really texting a friend or checking other social media. It can be difficult, but you have the discipline to do it.

POST HASTE

USING PERSONAL
SOCIAL MEDIA

Social-media stupidity can get people fired, even when it's not too high-profile. CNN featured a story on its website featuring a barista who was fired for blogging about how annoying his job was, and a California Pizza Kitchen employee who was fired for tweeting about his dislike for the restaurant chain's uniforms. Being stupid on social media, even if it's done on your own time, can have very real consequences.

In a 2014 survey, the law firm Proskauer Rose found that more than 52 percent of companies responding had dealt with an employee misusing social media. More than 71 percent of companies reported that they had taken disciplinary action against employees misusing social media. And 81 percent said that they saw misuse of social media by employees becoming more of a problem in the future.

Whether it's ridiculing bosses or other employees, making racist or sexist comments, posting embarrassing photos, or generally engaging in puerile banter, using social media as a way to vent your spleen is not only bad behavior—it can also get you reprimanded or fired. One solution might be to make sure that you use the settings to make any social media you use private and available only to those you approve. But even with security settings, there's no guarantee that a stupid post won't get out there. The true solution is to restrain yourself from posting anything stupid in the first place.

Social media can be a powerful business tool, too. You can use it to network with colleagues, live-tweet conferences and other professional events, and keep up with ongoing discussions in your field. With sites like LinkedIn, you can even use social media to find a job or make a hire.

But if you have an inappropriate observation to make, keep it to yourself. If you take a photo of you and your buddies inebriated at some event or another, don't post it. That shot of you taking a hit from a bong in college, which you somehow thought would make a fun Facebook profile photo? Take it down.

Even if you regret a post or tweet and decide to delete it, sometimes that's not enough. Once something makes its way to social media, all it takes is one person to grab a screenshot of it. Many teenagers have learned that even apps like SnapChat, which promises that photos or videos will disappear after viewing, don't stop others from saving screenshots of damning posts.

While one of the values of social media is the immediacy with which you can disseminate information, take a moment before posting to think about whether you truly want this information to represent you on the vast online community and whether you're ready to suffer the consequences of any and all backlash to the post.

Even what you perceive to be a "fun" post can wreak havoc.

Libby, a forty-something executive, was finding great success managing her department. Supervisors appreciated her vision. Employees liked working for her. Even colleagues from other departments also took a shine to her. She was able to manage her department and create strong ties to those running other departments.

One such ally was Seymour, the head of security for the organization. A former state police officer, Seymour offered to take Libby to a shooting range to teach her how to fire a pistol. Libby had never handled a firearm, nor had she had any desire to. But she thought it might be fun to give something new a try.

So they set up a time and met one another at the range. It was, she admitted, fun.

Before they finished, Seymour used his cell phone to snap a photo of Libby holding the gun. There she was with a big smile, two hands on the pistol held waist-high and pointing toward the floor. Seymour texted her a copy of the photo, and when she returned home that night, she made it her profile photo on Facebook.

Several weeks later, tragedy was in the news. A gunman had broken into a school and killed 20 children and 6 adults, then committed suicide by shooting himself.

For days, Libby's profile photo with the handgun remained on her Facebook page, visible to friends, family, and colleagues.

A friend and colleague, Ling, noticed the profile photo soon after Libby had posted it. When the shooting occurred, he checked Facebook to see if she was still using it. She was. Ling was concerned that she might face criticism over her judgment about using the photo.

As a friend and colleague of Libby's, what would you do?

A Nothing. Mind your own business. Stay uninvolved. If asked, plead ignorance.

B Report Libby to the human resources department for her questionable judgment.

C Call or e-mail Libby to ask if she might want to change the photo given the recent news.

D Screenshot the photo and tweet all about it.

E Alert local news media to see if they might sniff a story in the executive's decision to post the photo.

While Libby might have meant the photo to be humorous—and certainly didn't intend any malice—she didn't show the best of judgment posting it in the first place. Pistols and weapons had nothing to do with her job. The in-joke might have been lost on those viewing it. Once the shooting occurred, it made the photo appear to be in even poorer taste.

Ling had no desire to embarrass or cause trouble for Libby, so options B, D, and E hardly seemed the right approach. He wanted to help save her from potential embarrassment, so doing nothing (A) didn't seem right, either.

Ling messaged Libby on Facebook (C) and asked if she thought she might want to change her profile photo given the recent shooting tragedy and the heightened sensitivity toward attitudes about handguns.

"Yikes," she responded. "I hadn't even thought of it. You're totally right, and I appreciate it." She took the photo off of her page.

It's up to each of us to show good judgment in how we use social media. But if your business colleagues and friends show lapses, it's good to remind them that the whole online world could be watching.

_____

Even a fun post can wreak havoc.

_____

When you use social media, ask yourself these questions:

> Does this post portray me in a way I'd be embarrassed to be portrayed?
> Is this post vulgar?
> Does this post show me or friends in states that are best kept off the Internet?
> Am I criticizing my company or my colleagues publicly?
> Could my posts be construed as racist, sexist, homophobic, or otherwise derogatory toward a particular group of people?
> Have I thought through why I want to publish this?
> Am I being stupid?

WE HAVE TO STOP MEETING LIKE THIS

MEETINGS (AS A PARTICIPANT)

I'm not a fan of meetings, particularly unnecessary ones. Too often, they take up time that could be spent getting actual work done. Over the years, I've been to meetings where the only discussion was to ask everyone to check their schedules when they got back to their office to see if they could come up with dates about future meetings. I've also been to meetings where people were told—after they'd already arrived—that if they'd attended the same meeting the previous year, there really wasn't any reason for them to be at this meeting.

I firmly believe that meetings should be held only when there's a specific agenda and purpose. I also firmly believe that meetings should start on time and not be stretched out for any longer than they actually need to be.

When I was an editor at a magazine that targeted entrepreneurial companies, we ran a short piece about a manager who held meetings in a room without chairs. When people had to stand up, they were motivated to get to the point without taking any longer than necessary. Subsequent research performed at Washington

University in St. Louis (also reported in the magazine, years after I'd left) suggests that stand-up meetings also result in better creativity and teamwork. Such techniques may sound a little odd, but I'm willing to try anything that will keep meetings as focused and as short as humanly possible.

Of course, some meetings are necessary, and sometimes they can be productive, but research from software developer Atlassian suggests that an average of 31 hours is wasted in meetings every month, costing a staggering $37 billion in the salaries of those wasting time. Most employees, the research found, attended 62 meetings a month. Ugh.

A team at an organization providing health-care services had been meeting every Monday morning for years. It began as a way for them to update one another on cases or seek advice from team-mates about particularly thorny issues. For many months, the meetings worked well. People showed up on time, reported on their cases, discussed their work, advised one another, and then ended the meeting.

But then the manager who was charged with running the meet-ing, Rebecca, began to show up a few minutes late. No notice—she just arrived a few minutes late. As time went on, a few minutes grew to ten, and then the manager routinely showed up a half hour late to the meeting she was supposed to be running.

Because none of the team members knew if Rebecca would be on time or not, they showed up to the meeting and got down to work. But when she did arrive, they found themselves having to retrace their footsteps, repeating what they had already reported to one another or answering questions for Rebecca that had already been covered by the group.

Frustration grew. But the meetings continued, and Rebecca's erratic timeliness continued as well.

Since Rebecca technically outranked the other members of the team, they were at a loss about what to do. Many of them found the meeting time took away from time they could be spending with patients or completing other work. If Rebecca showed up on time, they'd be able to finish the meeting in half the time and get back to work.

Their first approach was to discuss the issue of Rebecca's tardiness at the beginning of one of their meetings. They decided to ask her if she would like them to move the meeting back by a half hour to accommodate her schedule. Rebecca responded that she didn't want to move the time of the meetings. She had them marked on her schedule and set aside time each week for them. She told them she would do her best to get to the meetings on time, but that they should be patient with her.

Weeks passed. Then months. Rebecca continued to be late, often by more than a half hour. She never made mention of her lateness when she arrived, and people continued to have to repeat what they'd already covered.

What would you do as a meeting attendee?

A Start coming to the meeting a half hour late yourself, hoping that Rebecca will never show up on time.

B Ask Rebecca again if she wants to change the time of the meeting to better accommodate everyone's schedule.

C Enlist the help of Rebecca's boss to see if the meetings are still necessary and to seek advice on how to better use the time.

D Just stop going to the meetings.

E Anytime Rebecca asks about something that was covered before she arrived, blast a loud air horn.

F Tell Rebecca she doesn't need to attend the meeting.

Hoping for the best (A) is not a strategy. Trying to anticipate whether or not Rebecca would be late would still produce redundant, inefficient meetings. Stopping attending the meetings (D) was an option, but given that the team members found real value in comparing notes, it would have been a choice based on Rebecca's annoying behavior rather than what was best for the team. An air horn (E) is something that an entrepreneurial owner might try in a startup—but then, an entrepreneurial owner would likely have little patience for persistent tardiness.

Asking Rebecca again to revisit the timing of the meetings (B) would be a good tactic, as would giving her the option of not attending the meetings if she doesn't really need to (F). But given the wasted time that could be spent focusing on the organization's core work, the team decided that going to Rebecca's boss with a proposal for a more productive way to run the meetings (C) was the best response. It ran the risk of annoying Rebecca, but if it were presented in a constructive way, the boss might see the wisdom in the approach.

If the boss pushed back on the team members and told them to work it out with Rebecca, then they would have to take it on themselves to make sure that there was a clear agenda for each meeting and to stick rigorously to that agenda. When Rebecca was late and asked some people to repeat themselves, it would be perfectly appropriate to tell her that they'd fill her in after the meeting if she'd like more detail. They could also assign someone the task of taking minutes that could be shared with anyone who had to miss a meeting. No one could force Rebecca to be on time, but her best response to this issue would be to plan ahead to prevent being late or to find a better time for the meeting.

Keep meetings as short
and as focused as humanly possible.

As a participant in a meeting, it's good form to do the following:

> Show up on time.
> Avoid using phones or tablets unless you're specifically using them to take notes about the meeting.
> Ask to see an agenda for the meeting.
> Don't interrupt others when they're talking.
> Seek out clarification if you don't understand what someone is trying to say.
> Stay on point and avoid veering into tangential topics.
> Bring any necessary papers or materials, and don't forget to take them with you when you leave.
> If you can't make a meeting that you'd said you'd attend, let the other attendees know.
> Avoid falling asleep or loudly yawning during the meeting.

THERE'S NO AUGGHH IN T-E-A-M

TEAMS
(AS A MEMBER)

"**M**any people act as if being a team player is the ultimate measure of one's worth, which it clearly is not," J. Richard Hackman, the author of *Leading Teams: Setting the Stage for Great Performances*, told *Harvard Business Review* editor Diane Coutu in a 2009 interview. "There are many things individuals can do better on their own, and they should not be penalized for it."

While teamwork is often thought to be the magic that will result in greater productivity and accomplishment, experts like Hackman, a professor of social and organizational psychology at Harvard, believe, based on the research, that a team's success depends on how well a team is conceived and run.

For teams to work, Hackman believes that five conditions must be met. The teams "must be real," with the leader making clear who is on the team. They must have "a compelling direction"; the leader must make clear what the shared goal of the team is. They must have "enabling structures" and "norms of conduct" that are clear to all members. They need "a supportive organization" where teamwork is clearly rewarded. And they need "expert coaching"—advice from experts in teamwork "at the beginning, midpoint, and end of a team project."

Unfortunately, as members of teams, many of us have had less than optimal experiences. While it's the team leader's role to make the team's direction and goals clear, very often we find ourselves frustrated by the lack of a clear vision, an imbalance in the contributions from all team members, and a fuzzy sense of what the actual purpose of a given team is.

Still, it's up to each individual to try to work well with others on any team.

A midsize nonprofit put together a search team to try to hire the next executive director of the organization. The members were chosen both for their perceived expertise and to try to ensure that as many stakeholders in the organization as possible were represented on the search committee. The chair of the board of trustees appointed one of the team members, Anand, as the team leader.

As the search commenced, Anand assigned some team members to write the job description and ad, while others were responsible for making a first pass at reading any applications that came in. Anand reassured the team members that he would be in touch with both groups to make sure that everyone knew what everyone else would be doing. He also set up weekly meetings so the committee members could brainstorm and check in with each other.

At the first meeting, Anand arrived a bit late with a case of cold drinks and a few bags of pretzels. There was no agenda available before or during the meeting, so when he asked the team, "Should we get started?" they sat there wondering what they were supposed to start in on. "How's the progress going?" he asked. Again, silence from the team.

Finally, someone asked what Anand hoped the team would accomplish at these weekly meetings. He responded that they were supposed to be good times to check in on everyone's progress. So the team members responsible for the job description and ad talked a bit about that. The members tasked with reading applications couldn't report on anything until the job ad was placed.

No timelines were set. There was no effort to involve the team members who were waiting for applications in the overall goal of the team, which was to identify and hire a new executive director.

A couple of weeks passed and, aside from consuming the drinks and snacks Anand brought each time, the team made little progress. Team members grew frustrated. But at each meeting, when they asked Anand to tell them what he hoped to accomplish at that particular meeting, his response was "to talk about the progress everyone had made in their respective tasks."

If you were one of the frustrated team members, what would you do?

A Stop attending the team meetings.

B Ask Anand for an agenda for each meeting.

C Recommend a clear timeline for tasks that would lead toward the goal of identifying and hiring an executive director.

D Ask the chair of the board what he was thinking when he appointed this jamoke team leader.

E Tell Anand that his choice of snacks simply isn't nourishing enough to help you get anything done.

Not attending the team meetings (A) might have saved the team members personal time, but it would do little to get the team back on track. If their goal was to get the team on track, then it would be reasonable for the team members to request an agenda for each meeting (B) so they could come prepared for work and lay out a clear timeline for tasks they need to complete together to accomplish their goals (C). It wouldn't have killed Anand to bring healthier snacks (E), but the best snack in the world would not compensate for lousy teamwork. It was not clear that knowing what the chair was thinking (D) would help get things on track either.

Better to take the time to clarify the committee's goals and the role of each team member established so they could reach those goals when they needed to reach them.

Ultimately, this search for an executive director failed. After some months, when a new board chair was in place, a new search team was established. This time, the board chair made the objectives and roles of each team member clear from the start and provided them with the coaching they needed to get the job done, which they did.

> Be clear about the team's goals and
> the team members' roles.

Sometimes, you'll find yourself on a well-functioning team. Sometimes you won't. But you never want to be the source of the malfunction. Here are some ways to avoid doing so:

> - Get clear on the goals of the team.
> - Get clear on the role of each member.
> - Get clear on your own role and obligations.
> - Always deliver what you promise the team you'll deliver.
> - Show up prepared when the team meets.
> - If you hit a roadblock, ask for clarification or guidance from other team members or coaches.
> - Hold other team members accountable for the work they're assigned.
> - Don't insist that your way is the only way. Contribute, listen, and collaborate.
> - Make sure that at the end of each team meeting you know what's expected of you and of other team members going forward.

ASK A BOSS

WHAT'S THE BEST OR WORST EXAMPLE YOU'VE SEEN OF USING SOCIAL MEDIA AT THE OFFICE?

Sam Baber, director of talent and development at Spredfast, a social-software platform based in Austin, Texas, believes that using social media to boost volunteering or fund-raising efforts for a cause "that a swarm of people can get behind" is the best use of personal social media he's seen. "International efforts (such as responding to natural disasters) rate the highest," he writes. (His is a global company.)

The worst example Baber can think of is when someone tried to embarrass another employee who had fallen asleep on a couch during work hours. The post went viral on the company's Facebook page, "leading to humiliation as well as executive assumptions that we should fire the person, which we didn't."

The worst use of personal social media that Ann Handley, chief content officer of MarketingProfs, has witnessed? Someone "posting on Facebook they were baking cupcakes when they were on deadline—while others in the company were waiting for work to be completed."

Then again, Handley once signed a $20,000 training contract with someone from a Fortune 100 company after he'd seen her half-joking tweet: A photo of a marketing-themed board game with the caption "Well this looks like a possible drinking game . . . Drink when someone says 'tactics' before 'strategy.'" (Really. You can look it up.)

PART THREE

RISING TO THE TOP

IN AN INTERVIEW with the editor of the *New Statesman* in 1939, Winston Churchill observed: "Criticism may not be agreeable, but it is necessary. It fulfills the same function as pain in the human body; it calls attention to the development of an unhealthy state of things. If it is heeded in time, danger may be averted; if it is suppressed, a fatal distemper may develop."

If you want to succeed in business—and avoid developing a fatal distemper—you must learn to receive and give criticism well. Criticism is too often perceived as a bludgeon meant to bring someone down. But when done correctly and with respect, criticism is how we learn to be better at what we're trying to do—and also how we can help make colleagues better at what they do.

We can never know everything about everything. Nor can we objectively judge all aspects of our own work. Relying on others to point out how we can do better is a crucial means of getting better at what we do.

To be effective in the workplace, you need to not just work well with others but also learn from them. The only way to rise to the top is to engage well with others.

Learning how to network well can give you perspective on your own career. It can also keep you aware of new opportunities. Good networking involves give and take—you can give advice, job leads, or anything else that you yourself would be happy to receive if the tables were turned.

Learning to conduct meetings efficiently, lead teams productively, and interview prospective new employees conscientiously will help define you as a colleague who can be counted on. You want to be a colleague who can be counted on. (Repeat this as a mantra if it helps.)

If you can learn how to comport yourself with integrity and respect in everything from asking for a raise to quitting a job, you increase your chances of creating an enjoyable and rewarding career. And who doesn't want that?

A HARD DAY'S NETWORK

NETWORKING

f you want to succeed at networking, think of it as a way to help others achieve a goal rather than a way to help yourself. Too many people who go about networking set out to connect with as many people as possible in an effort to see what those people can do for them. Networking should not be a selfish endeavor. If you want it to help you find new opportunities, expose you to new ideas, locate new employees, and generally enhance your business life, approach networking as something mutually beneficial.

If those with whom you're trying to network seem only to want something for themselves, dump them. A lopsided relationship yields little for you or for the other people you might connect that networking contact with.

I've never considered myself a great networker. It's rare that I reach out to others to ask them to introduce me to people who can help me or whom I can help in return. I don't belong to networking clubs or attend networking breakfasts or lunches or dinners. This is largely due to my own idiosyncratic dislike for meetings and being around large groups of people I don't know.

But I do regularly field requests from former colleagues, students, and friends who ask if I could introduce them to someone they think I might know or have access to. In such instances, I tell them that I'd be glad to try to make the introduction, but I request that they treat any meetings as informational and don't ask for jobs, money, or favors. Also, I ask them to be generous with their own contacts should others ask them for such introductions.

Experts used to believe that we were separated from any other person by only six degrees. (Read your Stanley Milgram and consult the oracle of Kevin Bacon for evidence.) But recently, researchers at Facebook and the University of Milan have suggested that social-media networks have brought that number down to four degrees of separation. In other words, if you really want to reach someone, it's likely you can find a connection with him or her in four people or less. (There are lots of complicated mathematical formulas to support this thesis. I'll spare you the details.)

A better question than "How can I network to connect with someone?" is "How can I build a relationship with someone that will benefit both of us?"

My cardinal rule of networking etiquette is this: Be as generous with your own time and expertise as you expect others to be with theirs, regardless of how early or late you are in your career.

Years ago, I had a position helping to run a small financial publishing company. When I left to strike out on my own as a writer, many of the editors and writers on staff stayed in touch with me. (Many of us are still in touch, in fact.)

Later, as one of the editors, "Steve," was preparing to leave the company, he sought out freelance work so he would have a running start when he left to pursue writing full-time on his own. We had worked closely together, so I didn't hesitate when he called to ask if I might introduce him to some of the editors with whom I was now working. Others gave him contacts as well, and ultimately, he built up enough freelance work that he could comfortably leave the publishing company to freelance full-time.

After he'd been out on his own for a year or so, a colleague named "Michelle" contacted me to ask if I could introduce her to anyone who might help her find writing assignments. I didn't hesitate to put her in touch with Steve, who had built up a healthy portfolio of clients for his work.

When Michelle and I spoke a few weeks later, I asked if she'd had any luck speaking with Steve. There was silence on the other end of the phone. Then: "He told me he couldn't help me because he didn't want to risk losing assignments that he might get himself."

Steve had no trouble asking me and others for access to our contacts, but he refused to help others when they sought the same thing. Clearly, he broke the cardinal rule of networking etiquette.

What would you do in my position?

(A) Call Steve and tell him he's dead to you.

(B) Refuse to accept Steve's calls.

(C) Call as many mutual colleagues as possible and report on Steve's behavior.

(D) Set up time to talk with Steve and tell him that just as you and others had helped him when he was getting started, you hoped and expected he would help others you sent his way.

(E) Revise your cardinal rule of networking etiquette to "Ask others what they can do for you, not what you can do for them."

Cutting off contact (A and B) and ceasing to supply Steve with any networking assistance was indeed an option. But it didn't suit my character, and I had no desire to punish him for his behavior. Neither did I feel like bad-mouthing him to mutual colleagues (C). I wasn't about to revise my cardinal rule (E), because it is, after all, a cardinal rule, and one that I still hold to be true.

Instead, I chose to speak with Steve, remind him of the leads and networking help I had provided, and ask if he could be more generous with his own time and expertise in the future (D). Neither Michelle nor I were trying to take work away from Steve. But we hoped that networking would provide others similar opportunities to the ones he had been given.

I don't know if Steve shifted gears because he saw the wisdom in helping others who might in turn help him one day, or if he decided to do so because he feared being cut off from information and leads that I and others had provided him in the past. But he did seem to embrace the cardinal rule of networking etiquette after that and began to be as generous with his own information as he expected others to be with theirs.

**Help others as you would want
others to help you.**

If you try to network with others, remember these guidelines:

> The cardinal rule of networking etiquette: Help others as you want others to help you.
> By all means, use social-media sites like LinkedIn to see if a direct contact might introduce you to someone he or she is connected to, but don't press the issue if your direct contact tells you he or she doesn't really know the person you're trying to reach all that well. (Friends on social media are not always all that close and sometimes don't know one another at all.)
> Don't go into a networking relationship asking for favors, jobs, or money. Think instead of building a relationship.
> If you expect others to be generous to you, be generous to them.
> Don't inundate new contacts with too much information and incessant e-mails, calls, or direct tweets.

> Be clear about why you're calling someone when you reach out to them. Asking for an informational interview is often a great way to start. But if you're really reaching out to them to see if they might introduce you to someone else in particular, don't pretend you're trying to do anything else. Just ask them.

> Be patient for any payoff. It may take weeks, months, or years. It may never come. But the beauty of networking is that a payoff often does come, sometimes when you least expect it, so play nicely.

LET'S GET CRITICAL

GIVING AND
RECEIVING CRITICISM

A magazine writer I once regularly edited shared with me an old piece of wisdom about the perfect editor-writer relationship. "The best writer," he said, "is one who hands in his copy and then goes off and gets hit by a train." The editor could then do whatever he or she wanted to the copy without having to engage in back-and-forth criticism with the writer.

Gruesome, perhaps. But his point was that the often prickly part of an editor-writer relationship is when the editor has to give feedback to a writer on his or her work and the writer has to receive it. In other words, there might be a lot less potential conflict if we didn't have to deal with people.

The same goes for the business world. Criticizing others and accepting criticism ourselves can create tense situations. If you think of criticism as only pointing out the flaws in someone else's work, then it is indeed a challenging task. But if criticism is instead understood to point out strengths and weaknesses, as I believe it should be, then it can become less of a confrontation and more of a collaborative effort to improve performance.

Still, it's no simple task. Some managers choose to avoid criticizing employees at all costs and hope they'll miraculously alter their performance, even if the employees don't have a clue that they're falling short. It's part of a manager's job to let employees know what's working and what's not. And it's part of an employee's job to listen to criticism and improve how they do their job.

Managing should be an active endeavor, and criticism should be a useful tool for both the manager and the employee.

But giving and receiving criticism takes thoughtfulness and time. Correcting someone else as a means of exhibiting your superiority is hardly productive (and suggests you might need a healthy dose of counseling). Bullying or cajoling others to do things your way doesn't build trust or provide an understanding of how or why things might be done differently.

The goal of criticism should always be to make things work better in order to achieve a common goal.

Jesse was a new employee at a small insurance brokerage. His boss, Taylor, hired Jesse right out of school to serve as an assistant who would handle everything from managing the office to fielding e-mail queries from existing or prospective customers. Taylor liked Jesse's manner when he interviewed for the job and perceived him to be a thoughtful person with a good eye for detail.

After Jesse received a bit of training on how the office worked and who the various other employees were, he settled into the job. The supply closet was always well stocked. Materials for meetings were prepared in a timely manner and included the proportion of visual material and text that Taylor had told Jesse she liked.

Months went by, and Jesse established a regular routine. He would arrive at the office, turn on his computer, and look at e-mails that had come in overnight from existing or prospective customers. If it was necessary, he'd route them on to a more senior person at the firm. Otherwise, he'd answer them himself, generally by adapting responses from a range of previous e-mails that had been sent about particular products or services the company offered. If the latter directly involved Taylor or another senior person, Jesse would copy that person on his response.

Over time, Taylor noticed that the quality of Jesse's e-mail responses to prospective clients was inconsistent. More often than not, the responses were clear, concise, informative, and well written. But occasionally, Taylor noticed that Jesse would be a bit more informal than she liked, leaving out pronouns in sentences, for example ("Got it. Will get back to you."), or not catching typographical errors or grammatical mistakes before he hit "Send."

Taylor liked the job Jesse was doing, but she didn't want prospective customers to receive anything but the most professional responses from her firm. She needed Jesse to take more time with these responses, but she didn't want to give him the impression that he was an utter screw-up or that his job was in jeopardy (at least not unless his overall performance actually deteriorated).

What would you do in Taylor's shoes?

A Insist that Jesse send a copy of every e-mail to you before he sends it to a prospective customer.

B Take away Jesse's computer.

C Set up a meeting with Jesse to discuss his overall performance. Talk about what he's been doing well and where he needs to pay more attention to detail.

D Send Jesse to a class on writing business e-mails.

E Fire Jesse and hire someone else to do the job.

Reading every piece of correspondence before Jesse sent it out (A) would not be a long-term solution to the issue. Taylor could offer to answer any questions Jesse had about grammar or style, but having two people do Jesse's job—rather than helping Jesse do his job better—wouldn't be a productive use of time. Taking away Jesse's computer (B) would present a problem if Taylor still wanted him to field customer e-mails. If no one had talked to Jesse about avoiding an informal tone and taking time to proofread his e-mails, it's unclear a class on writing business e-mails (D) would help. Devoting money and time to a class that might not be needed without first directly addressing the issue would be wasteful. I suppose firing Jesse (F) is an option, but it would be foolish to devote resources to hiring and training a new person who might not do as good a job as Jesse on all those other tasks.

The clear choice was C. Taylor set up a meeting with Jesse and went over both what he was doing well and her concerns about his e-mail responses.

If you were Jesse, what would you do after receiving this feedback?

A Start looking around for a new job.

B Argue that your reason for the informal tone is to create a bond with prospective customers.

C Tell Taylor that your keyboard sticks and your computer is old and you're doing the best you can, given your poor resources.

D Listen to Taylor, taking note of what's working and where Taylor thinks you need to improve.

E Quit.

If Jesse hated his job, he should have certainly looked around (A), but not simply because of Taylor's observations about his work. Quitting (E) over this meeting wouldn't do Jesse any good, either. Blaming the computer (C) would be childish. If the computer wasn't working, he should have told Taylor or someone else about it prior to this meeting. Changing up the tone of the e-mails without consulting Taylor (B) would show poor judgment.

Jesse wanted to learn to do the job better, so he listened to what Taylor had to say about what he was doing well and where he needed to improve (D), and then he made the effort to improve.

*Give and receive criticism as a way
to achieve a common goal.*

When you give criticism, here are some things to remember:

> Avoiding the issue only prolongs the problem.
> Be as constructive and specific as possible.
> Ask the person receiving the criticism if he or she understands what you're trying to tell him or her.
> If you have something positive to say about how the job is being done, say it.
> If you have something negative to say, provide solutions on how to improve performance.
> Make it clear that the criticism is not meant as a hint that the person's job is in jeopardy—unless it is. If it is, then make that clear as well.

And here are some things to remember if you're receiving criticism:

> Avoid making excuses or being defensive.
> Listen for ways in which you might do your job better.
> Ask for assistance if you believe you need it to do your job better.
> Ask for clarification if you don't understand what's being said.

If the goal of criticism is to make things work better in order to achieve a common goal, as it should be, then learning to give and receive criticism should be viewed as a positive experience, not something to be avoided at all costs.

MAKE MEETINGS MATTER

MEETINGS
(AS A LEADER)

L ooking back at a column I wrote years ago for a technology magazine on how to run an effective meeting, I'm struck by how the guidelines I offered then haven't changed. I'm also struck by just how awfully most meetings are run.

I hate meetings. I've attended too many meetings with unclear purposes or poor focus. Basic business etiquette seems to go out the window when it comes to running meetings. I do have colleagues who like meetings as a way to bring people together in one setting. That's an okay thing, but do we really need a meeting to do this? I'd rather be home having a nice piece of fish.

If you're called on to lead a meeting, you set the tone. How the meeting plays out depends a great deal on how you decide to run it. Being routinely late, for instance, sets a poor example and sends the message to others that it's okay to be late to your meetings. The least you can do if you're running a meeting is to show up on time.

But you should also do more than that. You should make sure that you need the meeting, that you invite the right people to the meeting, that you set a clear agenda for the meeting, and that you don't prolong the joy (almost wrote *agony*) any longer than you need to. If you have employees who live for meetings and never want to leave, then they may not have enough work to do or they may be using a meeting to avoid the work they should be doing.

Larry was not a fan of meetings either. But he knew their value and scheduled meetings with his colleagues whenever there was a particular task they needed to tackle together.

Larry tried to keep the attendance at his meetings as small as it needed to be. Before calling a meeting, he sent out a note to colleagues telling them that he'd like to meet with them and gauging when would be a convenient time for each of them. If all of them couldn't make the same time, he looked for a time when the majority could. He also told his colleagues, in broad strokes, what the meeting would be about, and asked them to let him know directly if they thought anyone else from the business would add value to the particular discussion. He promised to send out a more detailed agenda once the meeting time was established.

On one such occasion, all had gone as it typically did with Larry's meeting planning. He found a mutually agreeable time, added a couple of invites based on recommendations, and sent out a short agenda for the meeting, asking if colleagues could give some thought to each agenda item before arriving.

The meeting time came. Larry was there 10 minutes early to make sure that the overhead projector worked and that there were enough chairs in the room. He had some extra copies of the agenda with him as well.

When the meeting time hit, all but one person was seated and ready to meet. Larry began the meeting.

The latecomer, who was one of the people who had been recommended as an additional invite, arrived 15 minutes into the meeting. The discussion continued as the new arrival took his seat. The colleague sitting next to him handed him a copy of the agenda and pointed to the bullet item they were in the process of discussing.

Moments later, the latecomer chimed in, asking, "Could you bring me up to speed on where we are?"

Larry, no lover of meetings and a loather of lateness to meetings, paused for a moment. What would you do next?

A Ask the latecomer to leave the room immediately.

B Glare at the newcomer and ask, "Have you no sense of decency, sir?"

C Start the meeting from the top, asking other colleagues to provide a synopsis of how they had contributed to each of the bullet points already covered.

D Thank the newcomer for coming, tell him you'd rather not lose the thread of discussion, and say that you believe he'll be able to catch up on his own.

E Stand up, push your chair into the table, and walk out of the room.

While I know of at least one CEO who used to charge his employees $1 for every minute they were late to meetings, Larry had imposed no such mechanism. He thought it would be rude to ask the latecomer to leave (A) and just as rude to storm out himself (E). Questioning the newcomer's decency (B) would hardly be good etiquette, nor would it productively move the meeting along. Starting all over again (C)? A waste of everyone's time.

Because this was a meeting Larry called and therefore he was setting the tone, he chose to be polite to the latecomer but to keep the meeting on track (D). The newcomer might have been taken aback, but he was the one who breached business etiquette in the first place by showing up late, so he had no right to tell Larry how to run the meeting.

> If you're running the meeting,
> you set the tone.

If you're running a meeting, here are the guidelines I offered in that column years ago, along with some others:

> Be clear on your objective. Know what you want the meeting to accomplish and make that objective clear to the attendees beforehand.
> Have a clear agenda. Whenever possible, list the time allotment for each discussion as well as an overall start and finish time.
> Invite only the people who need to be at the meeting. Don't waste others' time.
> Start and finish on time.
> Make sure ahead of time that any technology and supplies you need at the meeting are in place and in working order.
> Remind everyone to turn off their cell phones.
> Conclude the meeting by clearly stating what next steps are needed.
> Never call a meeting that isn't essential. Don't waste people's time.
> Make it your personal goal in life to call as few meetings as possible. Doing so would be a sign of utmost human decency.

PULLING INTO THE LEAD

TEAMS
(AS A LEADER)

The key to being a good team leader is to get other members of your team to trust you and your leadership skills. If you've worked with your team members in the past, the ability to build this trust may be easy, or it may be quite hard, depending on their perception of you in the workplace. But if you're leading a team, you should do everything in your power to let the team know that you have their interests in mind when trying to accomplish whatever tasks the team is charged with accomplishing.

The team leader is responsible for making sure that the team works well together toward a common goal. The leader must keep the team's focus on the work to be done, not on the individual personalities in the group. No team leader should be expected to conduct a group therapy session. If therapy is needed, then employees seeking it should see what kind of coverage they have through the company's health benefits.

Throughout the task, the team leader must remember that whatever they're doing is to be a team effort. Sure, you can fall back on the clichéd wisdom that there's no *I* in TEAM, but that doesn't keep some members from focusing on the M and the E. Each *me* is part of a larger team effort, and it's the leader's job to make sure that everyone remembers that.

A company that sold shelving and other types of displays to retail stores was moving from one Midwestern state to another. The chief operating officer asked the warehouse supervisor, Alai, to lead a small team made up of the office manager, a top salesperson, a human resources representative, and an accounting-department executive. They were charged with developing a timeline that would help everyone in the company know who needed to pack and move what by when.

At the first meeting, Alai laid out the team's goal of creating a timeline for the move. The team looked at the company's organizational chart and was tasked with figuring out when each department should move based on how much physical equipment and how many people were involved. Alai asked if everyone was clear on the task to be completed by their next meeting a couple of days later. The team members had some general discussion but stayed focused on who would research which department. Alai thanked them each for their time and asked them to alert him if they ran into any roadblocks, and they dispersed.

At the follow-up meeting, everyone but the salesperson, Bart, came with copies of their initial assessments of what would be involved in the physical move. Bart sat quietly, not offering anything to the conversation.

Finally, Alai asked him, "How did your research go?"

Bart hesitated and then began to talk about how busy the past two days had been with orders and other sales tasks. When Alai asked him if he had prepared any research, Bart answered, "No."

What would you do in Alai's position?

A Tell Bart that he's an embarrassment to the company and that his lack of effort reflects poorly on him, his character, and his unborn children.

B Tell Bart that you understand how busy sales can be and offer to complete his part of the research for him.

C Ask Bart what he needs to get the research done and how long it will take.

D Ask Bart if he will complete his research by the end of the day and then share it with the rest of the group via e-mail.

E Report back to the COO that the company should delay the move since Bart is a screw-up.

Chewing Bart out (A) wouldn't solve much. A team leader should stay focused on the team's goal. Telling the COO that the move was a no-go because the team fell short of the mark (E) would not have been appropriate. Alai's job was to lead his team so that everyone contributed, not to do all the work himself, so B would be inefficient.

Alai decided to ask Bart to get the information to the rest of the team by a specific time (D). He could have also asked Bart what he needed to get the job done (C), as long as he set a specific deadline and held Bart to it. Alai clearly communicated to Bart and to the entire team that they needed to complete their tasks so that the move could happen as smoothly as possible.

If Bart still failed to produce after that clear communication, then Alai could assess whether he needed to reassign the task. But that should come only after Alai had made his best effort to get everyone to do what they'd committed to doing.

Ultimately, Bart contacted Alai right after the meeting, apologized for dropping the ball, told him how he planned to complete his part of the timeline research, and then delivered it to the entire group via e-mail the following morning. Never did Alai seek to embarrass Bart or chew him out in front of the team. He stayed focused on getting the team's goal accomplished, and the team moved on with its task from there.

As team leader, you have everyone's interests in mind.

Here are some key ways of showing good etiquette as a team leader:

> Build trust.
> Communicate clearly and well.
> Have and express a clear vision for the team's goals.
> Lay out clear expectations.
> Delegate.
> Listen to team members.
> Hold team members accountable to one another.
> Be honest.
> Be consistent.
> Show respect.
> Never take on the entire task of the team yourself.

PLEASE, SIR, MAY I HAVE SOME MORE?

ASKING FOR A RAISE

Salaries remain elusive, mysterious, and awkward at many companies. State-funded public institutions might make salaries public, and websites like Guidestar.org will tell you the salaries of top-paid employees at any nonprofit that files a 990 form with the IRS, but salaries at most companies are a big honking secret. The only way to know what the person in the office next to you makes is if the person in the office next to you tells you. Even then, you can never be sure if that information is entirely accurate.

Such secrecy makes it difficult for employees to know if they make as much as someone else doing the same job. It also lets some companies fail to address the pay disparities based on gender and race that continue to exist.

Still, asking for a raise based on what someone else makes at the company can be a risky gambit. For one thing, if the company considers the information confidential, your superiors might be suspicious about how you got the information. But more importantly, going in to the boss and demanding a raise based on what you think someone else makes sets up a confrontational situation from the get-go. Better to make a case for why you deserve a raise based on what you bring to the company, rather than trying to embarrass the boss into giving you a raise.

If a company is discriminating in its pay practices based on gender, race, or other issues, it should be held accountable. But in the short term, if you're asking for a raise, going in all confrontational is not likely to be in your best interest.

At Kyle's company, raises were offered once a year and were tied to annual performance reviews. Each employee would meet with his or her manager, go over how they performed the prior year, and talk about goals for the coming year. Then the conversation would end with the manager telling the employee what his or her raise was going to be, if anything.

The process always frustrated Kyle. He felt that tying the performance review to the salary discussion was a ridiculous waste of time. Few people, he assumed, cared what the boss had to say about goals and expectations when they were distracted by the knowledge that the money talk was coming at the end of the discussion. Still, this was the company's process, and Kyle was prepared for his annual discussions with the boss.

The company wasn't having its best year, and the word had gone out that all salary increases would be capped. Not everyone would get the cap, but employees were told that managers would not be permitted to give more than the cap.

But Janelle, a colleague from another department who'd already had her annual review, had told Kyle that she had been given a raise far greater than the cap that had been announced. She didn't tell Kyle this in confidence; she just mentioned it when he expressed frustration with the review process and disappointment that salaries would be capped in a year when he had performed exceptionally well.

When Kyle entered his manager Jerry's office, he was prepared to be positive and enthusiastic about the coming year. The performance-review part of the discussion went well. Jerry told Kyle how much he valued his contributions and pointed out some accomplishments that had been particularly notable. Not a negative word was spoken. The goals he laid out for the coming year were essentially to do more of the same and to keep up the strong work.

Then Jerry sighed and said, "Listen, I'm giving you the top of the cap for a raise this year. If there hadn't been a cap imposed throughout the company, I would have argued for a much more substantial raise based on your performance."

Kyle thanked Jerry, but of course, he knew what he knew about Janelle's raise. What would you do next?

A Hug Jerry and tell him that you know how hard this must be for him.

B Tell Jerry that with another kid about to enter college, you need far more money than the cap allows.

C Shed a single tear, stand up, and quietly exit Jerry's office.

D Tender your resignation.

E Thank Jerry again, but let him know that while you understand the constraints, a colleague in another department told you that she got a raise greater than the announced cap.

Bringing personal circumstances into the need for a larger raise (B) is inappropriate. Kyle should be paid for the work he brought to the company, regardless of whether he had 12 kids or 1. The job Kyle chose to take might be dictated by how much money he needed to support his family, but arguing that he should make more than others because he had more mouths to feed or tuitions to pay would have been inappropriate. There's no crying (C) in asking for a raise. And threatening to quit or actually quitting on the spot (D) when you don't get what you want is childish. Not getting what you believe you're worth might motivate you to start investigating

jobs elsewhere, but it should not be motivation to threaten or con-
front your boss. Rest assured that not getting more money is much
harder for the employee than for the manager giving him the news,
so no hugs (A) are needed. Generally speaking, avoid hugging your
boss during a performance review.

In the end, Kyle told his boss about the colleague whose raise
exceeded the cap (E). It was risky, because if Jerry had pressed the
issue and asked Kyle for her name, it could have put Janelle in an
awkward position. Kyle also needed to make sure that Jerry didn't
think he was calling him a liar or confronting him with an ultima-
tum. Instead, Kyle tried to present the information as something
Jerry might be able to use to get more for his employees if he chose
to do so. It could, of course, all backfire and create a rift between
Kyle and Jerry if it felt confrontational. But Kyle didn't threaten
to leave if he didn't get a larger raise. He didn't cry. He didn't hug
Jerry. He just told him what he believed to be true.

It was a risk that happened to pay off for Kyle. Jerry went to his
boss and discussed whether all departments were held to the same
cap. When it came out that they weren't, Jerry made a case for a
larger raise for some of his employees, Kyle being one of them.

Traditional etiquette might have called for Kyle to sit there and
take whatever Jerry offered, without commenting on his knowledge
of raises elsewhere in the company. But Kyle decided that presenting the information civilly and without threat was both honest and
worth a try. It would have been wrong to yell at Jerry and call him a
liar. Kyle wasn't docile, accepting whatever the boss doled out, but
he wasn't hostile about getting more, either. Good job, Kyle.

Make your case,
but don't be confrontational.

You might not always—or ever—have information that gives you the leverage to get a raise. But learning to ask for a raise well might help increase your chances of getting closer to the salary you want. Here are some dos and don'ts to remember while making the attempt:

> Establish your worth to the company. Make clear what you do, how well you do it, and how you plan to continue doing it there.

> Do some research into how comparable jobs pay in the industry, and if they pay more, use that information.

> If raises are given once a year and tied to performance reviews, make your case prior to your annual meeting. By the time the meeting rolls around, the salary decisions are likely already made and thus will be harder to change.

> Don't be confrontational.

> Don't bring your personal life into the discussion about salary.

> Reconsider asking for a raise if you know the company has just filed for bankruptcy.

> Don't threaten to quit on the spot if you don't get what you want.

> Don't whine.

> Don't cry.

> Don't hug your boss.

ENOUGH ABOUT ME, LET'S TALK ABOUT YOU

INTERVIEWING CANDIDATES

There are some things you can't legally ask prospective employees. I'm writing about etiquette here, not law, so if your HR department tells you not to ask some questions during a job interview because it's illegal to do so, listen to your HR department. (If it turns out your HR department is making stuff up, your company has bigger problems to deal with than interview questions.)

Generally speaking, you cannot legally ask people about specific personal issues (family, religion, race, disabilities, and so on), but you can and should focus on whether someone can perform the job you want him or her to perform. You also want to ask questions that let you see if the person would work well with your existing team.

The law and etiquette do overlap sometimes. It's not good etiquette, for example, to discriminate against a prospective employee because of gender, race, religion, family situation, disability, age, or any other issue that has nothing to do with the job you're trying to fill. Such discrimination is the type of bad etiquette that could and should land you or your company in legal trouble. Don't be a narrow-minded, racist, sexist, homophobic, anti-Semitic, ageist jerk when interviewing people. And try not to call people jerks. (My bad.)

Sheila was being wooed as one of several candidates to run a new department within a division of a large educational company, but after she applied, she didn't hear anything from the prospective employer. So Sheila was surprised when, a year later, she received an e-mail from the firm asking her if she was still interested in the position.

It gave Sheila pause that the search had dragged on for so long without any communication, but she was still interested. She liked her current work, but running her own department would be a step up in responsibility at a company that had a good deal of respect in the industry. Sheila replied to the e-mail and, within the week, set up a time to go across town to interview for the position.

When she arrived to meet with Kevin, the person heading the search within the division, Sheila was kept waiting in his assistant's office. Five minutes passed. Then 10. Finally, he came out, greeted her, and they entered his office. The interviewer described a bit about the company and the new position and then asked Sheila about her experience with such work. They were engaged in conversation when a beep came from Kevin's computer. He swiveled his desk chair and turned to respond to an e-mail that had just come in. "Sorry," he said. "I've been waiting on this one."

They began talking again. Sheila found Kevin interesting, and he seemed to take an interest in her work. They were interrupted by his cell phone, which he answered. It was clearly a personal call, and Sheila tried her best not to appear as awkward as she felt. When he hung up, they resumed talking.

Sheila did ask Kevin about the year that had passed since the position was first open. He indicated that they'd had some budgeting issues but that all was back on track now.

As they wrapped up their conversation, Sheila was shepherded to the office of the new division head, Luis, who had just started the job a few weeks before. He met with Sheila right away, and they discussed many of the same things Sheila had talked about with the first interviewer. Luis also walked Sheila around the offices to give her a sense of the workplace. He spoke a bit about his recent arrival and how he was still determining how best to run the division. They concluded their conversation, and Luis assured Sheila that he would be in touch.

A few weeks passed. During that time, Luis learned more about the search that began a year before and had been relaunched shortly before his hire. He discovered that there was disagreement within the division about whether the position Sheila was interviewing for was necessary. It appeared that Kevin had used the time between the former division head's departure and Luis's arrival to relaunch the search for the position, which he thought needed to be filled.

When Luis took the time to study the structure of his organization, the resources available, and the goals for the next several years, he decided that it didn't make sense to go forward with the hire of a new department head. Instead, he'd reallocate the responsibilities that person would have had to other managers within the division.

But Sheila, their prime candidate, was still waiting to hear from the company.

What would you do if you were Luis?

Ⓐ Nothing. Sheila waited a year without hearing anything. Why should she expect to hear anything now?

Ⓑ Ask your assistant to e-mail Sheila telling her that you won't be hiring her.

Ⓒ Call Sheila, apologize for the delay, and explain why the division has decided not to fill the position.

D Fire the first interviewer and give Sheila his job.

E Quit and return to your prior employer.

There are some points to consider before I get to what Luis did. Waiting a year to respond to an applicant for any job? Never good form. Making a prospective employee wait 10 minutes for a scheduled appointment and then answering e-mail and a phone call during the interview? No, no, no. No matter how good a conversationalist Kevin might have been, such rudeness is never acceptable. Sure, a prospect might be trying to impress you enough to get the job. But you're representing the company. Act accordingly. Kevin's behavior was rude enough that it's tempting to root for Luis to choose option D and fire the guy. But that's not a solution to this particular challenge (although Kevin might have it coming down the road).

Not giving Sheila any response (A) is bad form, not just because word gets around of how lousy a company treats its prospective employees (though that happens regularly), but also because it's wrong to treat others in a way that you would never want to be treated yourself. (See the "golden rule" variation in almost every organized religion.)

Luis might decide to quit and return to his former employer (E) if they'd have him, but that wouldn't solve this particular challenge.

He could ask his assistant or someone from HR to do the dirty work (B), but that would be the weaselly choice. Try to avoid being a weasel in the workplace. Besides, Luis thought Sheila was a strong candidate, and he didn't want to send her any other impression.

Good etiquette here required Luis to engage in the awkward task of calling Sheila and letting her know that the position for which she had interviewed no longer existed and thus would not be filled (C). He explained to Sheila that this had nothing to do with her qualifications but rather reflected the recent change in management and decisions about the division structure. He also apologized that it took over a year to sort this all out, even though he wasn't on board when that delay occurred.

Sheila might have been disappointed. She might have been angry. But by moving quickly and being clear and honest, Luis did right by Sheila. It was unlikely that she'd want to pursue a future with the company again, but at least Luis didn't exacerbate the issue by adding to the delays or rudeness Sheila experienced from others at the company.

Show prospective employees the same respect you'd like them to show you.

If you're the interviewer, it's sound business etiquette to treat every prospective employee with courtesy and respect. You might know early in the interview that he or she doesn't have the qualifications you're looking for, but you should still treat him or her respectfully. You should be representing yourself and your company as well as you would hope the prospective employee would be representing him- or herself. Here are some pointers:

> Don't be dismissive with or judgmental about the prospective employee. Do your job and interview the prospect so you get a sense of whether they might be a good fit.

> Don't be unresponsive. If the applicants don't get the job or an interview, tell them. Some prospects you don't hire this time around might prove to be good employees later. Don't treat them rudely.

> Listen when a prospective employee talks. Don't cut him or her off. You're trying to get as clear a sense as possible of whether this prospect will be a good fit for the open position.

> Don't be late. You don't want to be kept waiting by the prospect, so don't keep him or her waiting.

> Be prepared. Read the prospect's résumé. Go over the job description. Talk to colleagues about the line of

questioning each of you will pursue. Don't try to wing it when the prospect walks in the door.

> Be honest. Don't lie about anything or offer fabricated information. Answer questions as transparently and honestly as you can. If you don't know the answer to a question, "I don't know" is the appropriate response.

> Don't be rude. Pay attention to the prospect. Don't allow yourself to be distracted by anything else during your time together.

> Be clear about when you'll get back to the prospect with information about the job.

> Don't eat in front of prospects while you're interviewing them, unless you are interviewing them over a meal and they're eating as well.

> Don't respond to e-mails during the interview.

> Turn off your cell phone during the interview.

> Remember to talk about your company and the position so the prospect has a good sense of the place and the job.

> Don't be a weasel.

CALLING A FOUL ON FOUL PLAY

INTERACTING WITH OTHER COMPANIES

No business is an island. It's a given that anyone engaged in business will work with or compete against other companies. But while anyone worth his or her salt wants to succeed, doing so at the expense of a competitor is not the way to go. If your company can't succeed on the merits of the products or services it offers and the strength of its employees, then you need to improve from within rather than painting your competitors in a bad light so you'll look better.

Fight your competitors fairly for customers. You might even consider providing a competitor with information as long as it's not proprietary. You'll have many opportunities to trash-talk competitors—trying to lure employees in, trying to steal away customers—but fight the urge. Have faith that what you have to offer is sufficient, and that your business can succeed without having to tear down a competitor. What customer or prospective employee would want to work with you if your chief strategy seems to be bad-mouthing your competitors? That's hardly a unique competitive advantage. Play hard, but play fair.

In the late 1990s, I wrote a column about a large textile firm that regularly hired student interns. The firm was well known and well regarded. It had been featured in one of the bestselling business books of the day as a company with a particular passion for excellence. The company prided itself on using the best ideas it could find to run the business. The chairman's often-repeated mantra was "Steal shamelessly."

Early on, this mantra effectively combated the long-held notion that a company shouldn't use any techniques or ideas that weren't invented by the company itself. It was designed to encourage employees to search for the best practices and incorporate them into the company's operations wherever possible.

Then something happened that seemed to take the idea too far. A smaller textile firm's CEO—I'll call him "Michael"—claimed that his company had been the victim of corporate espionage. He accused the larger textile firm of hiring one person to pose as a prospective investor and another to pose as a graduate student in order to gain access to the smaller firm's trade secrets.

The larger textile firm denied any wrongdoing, stating that its policies had always forbidden employees from trying to get proprietary information from competitors illegally.

Michael believed that by encouraging employees to "steal shamelessly," the larger company sent a message that anything was fair game when trying to get a leg up on competitors, even if it crossed an ethical and legal line. "When you take something that has negative connotations, just the subliminal message you send to your culture is different," he told me at the time.

While it's become commonplace for companies to share good practices and benchmark themselves against such practices, companies should be able to choose what to share and when.

The author of the book that profiled the larger textile firm told me that "the good news is that people love to share stuff." But the problem, I observed at the time, was that if even one employee took the phrase *steal shamelessly* too literally, "the rally cry can seem like a dirty-tricks license."

Feeling wronged, Michael had to decide how to respond to what he believed was corporate espionage, rather than a harmless borrowing of publicly known best practices. What would you do?

(A) Hire a graduate student of your own to pose as someone looking for an internship at the larger company so that you can "steal shamelessly" yourself.

(B) Sue the larger company.

(C) Use the incident as a lesson that you need to be more scrupulous in doing background checks on prospective investors, interns, and employees.

(D) Start feeding bad information to the larger company, hoping that it will continue to steal shamelessly but put these fabricated bad ideas into practice.

(E) Begin a shaming campaign by using advertising, public relations, word of mouth, and all methods available to spread word far and wide of what you think of the larger company.

Hiring his own spy (A) was not a good solution, because it would have put Michael's company in the same category as the larger company. By starting a campaign to bad-mouth the larger company (E), the smaller company would have taken the focus off presenting its own products as exemplary. It would have risked being perceived as a company that spends too much time spreading negativity and too little time focusing on the good it can provide to customers. Feeding bad information to the larger company (D) would be petty and, given that the smaller company had already made its accusation public, unlikely to work. It would also be bad business to devote resources to such subterfuge instead of to making the best products possible. Chalking the experience up to a lesson learned (C) may appear to be taking the high road, but c'mon, Michael believed his company had been wronged, and damagingly so. Sitting back would send a message that others could do to the smaller company the same thing that the larger company allegedly did. Putting itself in the role of victim without attempting to address the issue would risk hurting the company's reputation with customers and prospective employees.

So Michael chose option B: to sue the company. This move sent a loud and clear message: Do not deal unfairly with us. We will take action.

Threatening lawsuits regularly without cause shows no business etiquette. It's a distraction from doing good business. But taking legal action when you believe someone else has broached both etiquette and the law can be a legitimate and useful option.

Ultimately, the companies settled the lawsuit out of court. In spite of the settlement, the larger company that had allegedly stolen ideas from the smaller company continued to deny it had done anything wrong.

<hr>

Play hard, but play fair.

<hr>

When interacting with other companies, remember these tips:

> Play fairly.
> Cooperate, so long as cooperating doesn't interfere with getting your own business done.
> Do not bad-mouth competitors to prospective customers, employees, or others.
> Do not steal information from competitors.
> If you lose business to a competitor, focus on winning the next time rather than moping or engaging in trash talk.
> If you win business over competitors, don't lord it over them. Be as gracious in victory as you are in defeat.
> Do not take metaphorical aphorisms about competing— e.g., "Steal shamelessly"—too literally.

QUITTING TIME

QUITTING

In 1977, Johnny Paycheck had a hit country song called "Take This Job and Shove It," about quitting a low-paying job where the foreman is a "regular dog" and the line boss is a fool who thinks his flattop haircut is cool. It's a fun ditty, but if you decide to leave your job, don't sing about it—no matter how epic your line boss's haircut is.

What Paycheck tapped into (I'm guessing here, since my exegetical skills with respect to country-music lyrics are limited) was the desire that many people feel from time to time to tell a rotten employer how they've done you wrong over the years. With a new job offer in hand, that desire might be magnified. Fight the urge. When quitting any job, try to be as gracious as possible and don't burn any bridges, even if in the moment you can't imagine ever crossing back over that bridge.

I once quit a job at a company to which I later returned. When I left, I had no intention of ever going back. But the opportunity arose, and even though I'd been eager to leave when I did, I'd left on good enough terms that I could come back. In all honesty, I'm not sure I took such a high road the second time I left. I didn't speak badly of anyone, I didn't spread idle gossip, and I gave ample notice, but it was clear to both me and my employer that I was more than ready to leave for good. It would have taken little effort on my part to try to maintain a stronger relationship with my former employer, and I regret not doing so, even though I never worked for that company again.

Charlene had felt stagnant in her job for quite a while. Her boss was demanding, the work had become tedious, and there was little indication that her responsibilities would change anytime soon. She'd put out some feelers for jobs a year or so earlier, but nothing had led anywhere. So she stayed and stagnated some more.

Charlene had seen how angry her boss, Leon, became when other colleagues gave notice. She also saw what happened to some former colleagues who had used him as a reference: Once he knew they were looking for a job elsewhere, Leon never seemed to treat them the same. He placed more demands on them or was even tougher than usual in judging their work.

But now Charlene was getting some traction in her job search. She was told she was one of three finalists for a position she wanted. She took personal time to go on an interview, where she was asked for the names of three references. She was concerned that if she listed Leon as a reference and didn't get the new job, she'd be stuck in her current job with him treating her even worse than usual. But Leon was also the person best qualified to talk about her performance at her current job.

If you were in Charlene's place, what would you do?

A List Leon as a reference, give him a heads-up that he might be called, and hope for the best.

B Ask your brother-in-law to pretend to be your current boss, give his number to the prospective employer, and hope that no one will catch on to the ruse.

C Ask other colleagues within the organization to serve as references, explaining to the prospective employer that you're not yet prepared to let your current boss know you're searching for a new job.

D List Leon as a reference but don't warn him that he might be called, hoping that the prospective new employer won't call your references unless they're going to offer you the job.

E Tell the prospective employer that your current boss will punish you relentlessly if he finds out that you're applying for a new job.

Asking your brother-in-law to cover for you by pretending to be your boss (B) would be ridiculous, dishonest, and silly. "Don't make stuff up" is a cardinal rule of business etiquette and life. Speaking harshly about her current boss (E) may have reflected Charlene's true feelings, but it's bad form to bad-mouth a prior employer to a new employer. For one thing, you risk coming off as a kvetcher. No one likes a kvetcher. For another, your indiscretion may send a signal to the prospective employer that you're, well, indiscreet. How will you talk about the prospective boss if he should offer you the job? Telling Leon that he was given as a reference (A) would have been an honest approach, but Charlene knew that if she didn't get the job, Leon would likely treat her differently at work. But not giving him a heads-up at all (D) would be unprofessional. You should always ask those you want to use as references if they're willing to do it and let them know that they might be called.

Because Charlene was concerned about signaling her job search to her current boss, she decided that asking other colleagues to serve as references (C) was an appropriate and fair way to go. Without saying anything bad about Leon, she also explained her reasoning to the prospective employer in hopes that he'd honor her decision to use these particular references.

Don't burn your bridges.

When quitting a job, try to do the following:

> Leave on terms that are as positive as possible.

> If you have an exit interview, don't spend a great deal of time grousing about your current job or boss. If your boss was truly abusive, you should have taken that up with HR while you were still on the job. Emphasize what you got from the job and leave it at that. (If a boss is truly abusive—and not just someone who doesn't happen to be to your taste—report him or her. But remember to distinguish between annoyance and abuse. You can live with annoying until you find a new job or figure out a way to manage the irritation.)

> Give sufficient notice. It used to be that two weeks was standard. If you're involved in a large project and it will take weeks to find a replacement for you, you might consider giving more notice. Don't leave your company in the lurch.

> Don't bad-mouth your former employer to your new employer

> Don't truth-dump on your current boss with all the reasons you're leaving. Just tell him or her that you've been offered a new position and when you plan to leave.

> Don't cry.

> Don't e-mail your resignation, leave a voicemail, or text your boss to tell him or her you're leaving. Quit in person.

> Don't yell.

> Don't remind your boss about all the rotten things he or she did to you or others during your time there.

> Thank your boss if you appreciated the position and believe you learned something on the job. You may want to use him or her (or others at your current company) as a reference for another job down the road.

> Burn no bridges.

ASK A BOSS

WHAT'S THE BEST OR WORST WAY SOMEONE HAS ASKED YOU FOR A RAISE?

Mike Hofman, executive digital director at *GQ*, says that the best way he's been asked for a raise was an employee "telling me months in advance that she would like a pay increase and asking me how she might get to that level." For Hofman, that approach was "very professional and realistic." The worst? "Asking me a week into a new gig, when I was still evaluating who I wanted to keep let alone give more money to."

Dave Hills, CEO of San Francisco technology company Twelvefold, says that the worst request he ever got for a pay raise was a note slipped under his door by an employee, saying that a competitor had offered him a job with a higher salary. If it wasn't matched, the employee wrote, he'd quit. Hills quickly responded. "He got a note slipped under his door wishing him well at his new company."

PART FOUR

THE TRICKY STUFF

LIFE AT WORK can get messy. If you could just work for yourself *and* be your own customer, then you'd never have to worry about awkward situations where other people's feelings, beliefs, actions, and general folderol must be managed. But you always work with other people in one way or another. If you don't want to leave work every day with a banging headache or wake up dreading interaction with your colleagues, you have to find a way to manage the tricky, tangential-seeming stuff as well as you manage your actual job.

You can have friendships at work without forgetting your responsibilities as a colleague. You can understand that when people—even management—do things with which you don't agree, that doesn't make them idiots. (Calling them names, however, might put you in the idiot category, or it might even make you a bully. Whatever the case, neither an idiot nor a bully be.) You can learn to manage personal conflicts as gracefully as possible.

You can also accept the fact that not everyone is exactly like you. Cultures differ. Belief systems differ. It's critical to understand what these differences are and how they affect business relationships if you want to avoid embarrassing faux pas and work well with others.

After all, if you can't work well with others, something clearly isn't working.

IN THE EVENT OF AN EVENT

WORK PARTIES

A work party? What?! You work with these people all week and now you're expected to party with them as well? The madness never ends.

But work parties are a given at most companies, whether they're at a function hall or at the home of one of your coworkers. At these events, be gracious, don't overindulge, and remember that these are not the raucous college parties you might have enjoyed in your youth.

Galvin was a top manager at his company. He and his spouse, Terry, owned a large home in the city and regularly hosted a holiday open house for coworkers sometime in early January. All Galvin's coworkers and their respective partners were invited to the function, which was catered with good food as well as wine and beer. The annual invite put the hours for the soiree between 6:00 and 10:00 p.m.

For years, the party was a hit. It was a lot of work for Galvin and Terry, but they enjoyed hosting Galvin's colleagues outside of a work environment. Guests arrived, mingled, ate, drank, and often brought a small gift like a bottle of wine or candy to show their appreciation for the hosts.

This particular winter had been a tough one. Snow had been steady, often making it challenging to get to work and then get home. Finally, there was a break in the storms and the evening of the party was predicted to have glorious weather.

A few guests arrived right at 6:00 p.m., and the traffic picked up until coworkers were arriving in full force by 7:15. Food was put out and conversations struck up. More coworkers came. Some guests left by 8:30, claiming other commitments. By 9:30, the attendees had lessened to a few.

But right at 9:45 p.m., Alice and her partner arrived with a couple of nonwork friends in tow. Galvin was surprised by their late arrival, but he figured they'd just stopped in for a few minutes to make an appearance. Ten o'clock came and went. All the guests but Alice and her crew had left. They stayed and continued to drink and talk, mostly to one another, in Galvin and Terry's kitchen. Galvin and Terry began to pick up the plates and glasses left around by departed guests.

When 11:00 hit, Galvin began to get a bit annoyed, although it was difficult to tell since he was a notoriously even-tempered fellow.

What would you say to the guests who wouldn't leave?

Ⓐ "Please go."

Ⓑ "It would be so nice if you weren't here."

Ⓒ "Alice, did you get the invite that said six to ten?"

Ⓓ "Terry, I'm going out for a cigarette. Can you entertain these people?"

Ⓔ Nothing.

It was not Galvin's style to bolt, leaving his spouse to deal with the guests who wouldn't leave (D). Nor was it his manner to be ungracious and make Alice and her friends feel unwelcome (A, B, C), even if Alice had brought uninvited guests and stayed well beyond the end of the party. Alice failed to pick up on cues that no one else was there and that Galvin and Terry had begun to clean up the joint. Not wanting to respond to a lack of grace with a lack of grace, Galvin chose to be a good host and did nothing (E) to indicate to Alice that she and her minions were welcome to leave.

Finally, around midnight, Alice, her partner, and their friends left, leaving Galvin and Terry to clean up.

The following year, Galvin and Terry decided to take a break from hosting the annual office party. No complaints. No mention of why. Just a decision, based on the prior year's experience, that it would be good to take a break from hosting for a bit. Thank you, Alice.

Perhaps Galvin should have said something to Alice. It would not have been inappropriate for him to let her know that it had been a long day for him and Terry and that they were ready to call it a night. But Galvin was not in the wrong here. Alice was.

Never bring uninvited guests to an office party. Never overstay your invite or show up 15 minutes before the party's end time. Never be Alice.

Have fun, but stay professional.

Here are some tips to remember when you go to a work party:

> Don't drink too much.
> Don't eat too much.
> Dress appropriately.
> Respond to RSVPs if they are given, even if it's to indicate that you can't make it.
> Don't RSVP that you'll attend and then not show up.

> Make certain that spouses or partners are welcome before bringing them to any party.
> Don't be a mope. It's a party. Act as though you like being at a party.
> Consider bringing a small gift if the party is at someone's home.
> Try to mingle.
> Don't challenge that guy in accounting to a duel.
> Thank the hosts.

I HAVE A CLOSET FULL OF FRIENDS AT HOME

FRIENDSHIPS

Do not assume that your work colleagues are your close friends. And don't feel the need to let them assume you're a close friend of theirs who wants to hear their personal confessions or help them straighten out the entanglements of their personal journey. I'm not suggesting that you be rude or cold or indifferent to your work colleagues. But it's never good to assume that work is where you go to make close personal friendships that will last forever. That you should plan to do on your own time—if you have any.

In a *New York Times* op-ed, Wharton professor Adam Grant referenced research at the University of Georgia that suggested jobs "are more satisfying when they provide opportunities to form friendships." Sometimes you luck out and you do strike up a friendship with someone at work. But you should recognize that the purpose of going to work is to do your job, support your colleagues, and add to society by making a living—not to fulfill your personal desire for close relationships. For most people these days, moving from one job to another over the course of a career is the norm. It's tough to form and keep close friendships if you're moving on regularly and quickly.

One of my closest friends is someone I worked with many years (and many jobs) ago. But as for most of my other coworkers from previous jobs, in spite of the fact that I respected and enjoyed working with them, I'd be hard-pressed to remember all their names or where they are now. They were great colleagues, not close friends. You should treat your work colleagues well and expect the same from them. Any close friendships that evolve beyond that are a bonus.

Marty enjoyed his job and his colleagues. They worked hard, treated one another with respect, and enjoyed their jobs as well. Barry seemed to love his job, too. He and Marty worked on several projects together. Both drew the praise of their customers and their boss.

Often, Martin and Barry would grab lunch when they were working on a project together and exchange e-mails throughout the day updating one another on joint projects. On a couple of occasions, they went to a ball game together, and their families joined together for a Sunday picnic in the park once or twice.

After Marty left the company for a new job, he rarely reached out to Barry. Occasionally, Barry would e-mail Marty to ask him how the new job was going. Marty would typically reply with a terse "Thanks for asking. All's well here."

"Great," Barry would respond. "Maybe we can grab a drink sometime to catch up. Lots of stuff going on with the family. All good."

Marty would typically respond with a variation on "Take care, Barry. Thanks for checking in."

Over time, Barry began to grow annoyed that Marty didn't seem to want to catch up. They had worked so well together. They'd socialized. Their families had spent time together. Why was Marty dissing him so?

A Marty was a sociopath who used people and discarded them once they were no longer of use to him and his desire for power.

B Barry should have picked up on the signals that Marty didn't care for him all that much. He did, after all, invite him to baseball games only when the last-place team was in town.

C Marty clearly had been covering up his inability to use Google or Outlook calendar from everyone. Trying to set a time to meet Barry would confirm his technological ineptitude.

D That time Barry got the last parking space in the employee lot, leaving Marty to park on the street? Payback.

E Barry was confusing a good colleague with a close friend. He and Marty worked well together, but their relationship was that of good colleagues. That relationship changed once Marty moved to a new job. You can't force friendship.

Marty was not a sociopath (A), nor was he sending Barry signals about past feelings (B, D). Marty might have had a technological issue with his online calendar (C), but that's not what was going on here.

Marty wasn't dissing Barry. But clearly Barry believed that their relationship was more than one of good colleagues in the workplace (E). Marty likely didn't. That Marty still responded to Barry's e-mails checking in is an indication that he wasn't dissing him. He, like some people, just didn't want to go out for drinks. Eventually, Barry learned to leave it alone. He remembered all the good work they did together and stopped trying to turn a relationship with a former colleague into the bestest friendship of all time.

Sometimes you will make lasting friendships at work, but don't take a job with that expectation in mind. Having good colleagues you can count on to do good work with you is a great outcome. Go into any job working toward that, and you're far less likely to be disappointed when a good colleague doesn't want to be your close buddy.

**It's great if you strike up a friendship
at work, but don't expect one.**

Here are some things to remember about workplace friendships:

> Don't expect your work colleagues to confide their personal issues to you as a friend would.
> Don't expect to confide your personal issues to them.
> If a colleague doesn't want to socialize after work, don't make more of it than it is. Appreciate a good colleague for being a good colleague.
> If you're looking to make friends, use your personal life to do so.
> Don't pester colleagues with personal e-mails.
> If a colleague doesn't want to be close personal friends, don't infer that he or she doesn't like working with you.
> Do your job and let your colleagues do theirs. It is not their job to be your friend. You want a good, supportive colleague.

PLEASE STOP SENDING ME PENS

GIFTS

Being gracious is a good goal. Giving a gift can sometimes be a signal of such grace. When a colleague hosts a party at his or her house, bringing a small gift can be perfectly appropriate. But if you want to soften up your boss for a raise, giving him that 1915-S wheat penny he always wanted for his collection is way inappropriate. If your entire department wants to chip in to buy the boss a collective gift, that is far more appropriate than doing so on your own.

It's okay to give a gift to an assistant to recognize the support you've received over the year. But refrain from making the gifts extravagant or personal. You know what extravagant and personal means. A nice book or a tasteful plant for his or her desk shows appreciation enough.

When you give a gift, don't expect anything in return. Give a gift only because you want to show appreciation to someone with whom you work.

Many companies have informal or formal policies about employees receiving gifts from those they do business with outside of the company. While some companies permit their employees to receive outside gifts, a survey in 2013 by SAI Global Compliance found that of the 299 North American companies surveyed, 35 percent put a cap on the value of gifts received from outsiders at $25 or less. Seventeen percent of the companies surveyed do not permit their employees to receive gifts at all. One former employer of mine had an informal policy for a time that said you could never accept anything that you couldn't eat in one sitting, which seemed a bit unfair to those with lighter appetites.

I've always thought that instead of giving gifts, businesses should pass the savings of what they would have spent on those gifts to all of their customers. I'd much prefer $25 off my bill than a pen with your logo on it. No offense.

In any case, companies should make clear what their policies are about giving and receiving gifts to both employees and outside vendors.

Several years ago, I wrote about the founder of a service company who decided to show appreciation for her clients by sending each of them a $50 American Express gift card at holiday time in December. The note sent with the cards read, "For all the evenings spent at work, please enjoy an evening out on us." (It was several years ago, when $50 went a longer way toward funding a night out.)

Within days, two of the recipients sent the gift cards back with notes indicating that accepting them would violate their companies' policies about gift giving.

Needless to say, the founder of the service company was embarrassed.

What would you do to avoid such embarrassment?

Ⓐ Not send gifts to anyone. What a thoughtless gesture.

Ⓑ Make sure to check if the companies you're sending gifts to have gift-giving policies before deciding what to send, if anything.

C Send the gifts anonymously. How can you return an anonymous gift?

D Find out the cap for gifts and then break the gift into smaller increments to dole out over time to circumvent the spirit if not the letter of the policy.

E Next time, send pens.

The founder's gesture was not thoughtless (A). She really did want to send a message to clients about how much she appreciated the hard work they'd done. Sending an anonymous gift (B) would do something, but it wouldn't send the message that this founder in particular wanted them to know how much she appreciated their hard work. Sending pens (E) or other imprinted items might be an option, unless, of course, they were really expensive pens and still violated the clients' gift policies. As for option D, even I'm lost trying to figure out how to do what I've proposed.

If the founder wanted to send gifts, she should have made sure to check whether any of the recipient companies had gift policies (B). That would have saved her any embarrassment she felt and saved the recipients the time it took to return the gifts. Or she could have just done what Wal-Mart has done since its founding in 1962 and ban all gifts and gratuities, regardless of the value.

Follow company rules when giving gifts.

If you're giving a gift to an employee or another company, remember these pointers:

> Avoid making it too extravagant.
> Avoid making it too personal.
> Avoid using it to soften up a boss.
> Make sure you're not violating any company policy about gift giving.

If you're offered gifts from other employees or vendors, keep these tips in mind:

> Make sure doing so doesn't violate company policy.
> Do not solicit such gifts.
> Do not show favor to a vendor solely because you receive a personal gift that doesn't violate company policy.

Like I said, in my ideal world, all companies would establish a policy of no gift giving. That would avoid conflicts, embarrassment, perceived inequities, and agita in the workplace. But the business world is what the business world is, so if you must give gifts, do your homework before embarrassing yourself or the recipient by giving a gift that is forbidden.

SETTLING
YOUR
AFFAIRS

WORKPLACE ROMANCE

G enerally speaking, having sex in the workplace is a bad idea, even among consenting adults. But workplace romances will occur, and when they do, companies have a challenging time figuring out what, if anything, they should do or say about them.

The Society for Human Resource Management (SHRM) does an annual "workplace romance" survey to assess what kinds of policies companies have about workers in romantic relationships with each other. Fifty-four percent of workplaces do not have a verbal or written policy regarding workplace romances. Of those companies that do have a policy, 99 percent forbid relationships between a supervisor and a direct report, and 35 percent of companies even forbid relationships between employees who have the same supervisor.

It might come as a surprise that so many companies don't have formal or informal policies about romance in the workplace. But in an ethics column I wrote back in September of 1998 about workplace romances, I cited the same SHRM survey (well, an older version of it), and back then, 72 percent of HR professionals reported that their companies had no such policies. The most likely outcome of workplace romances back then, they said, was marriage.

Now, 40 percent of companies say they've received complaints over the past five years about favoritism from the coworkers of those engaged in workplace romances. Twenty-three percent reported claims of sexual harassment.

"Love contracts" were a relatively new thing back in 1998. These were documents in which coworkers were required to disclose their relationship and indicate that they freely entered into the relationship with the other person. Today, 5 percent of companies say they use love contracts, while 75 percent think that all love contracts do is incentivize lovers to hide their romance from others in the workplace.

Given that we spend so much of our waking hours in the workplace, it's ridiculous to believe that all romance can be squelched, no matter how strongly a policy is pronounced. The goal for companies is to make sure that no one is being harassed or compelled to enter into a relationship they do not want. No one should be allowed to use a relationship to curry favor with a superior or demand a relationship in exchange for favorable reviews. In a relationship where one person outranks the other, it makes sense for both parties to disclose that relationship to HR. Both parties should be protected from any sort of hinkiness should the relationship go sour.

Proper etiquette for a workplace relationship comes down to a pretty basic rule of thumb: Do not let your relationship interfere in any way with you or others getting your work done. Don't expect coworkers to get caught up in your romance. Avoid putting them in a position where they might have to do so.

Marion, 25, was a supervisor in a retail shop. She was responsible for taking inventory, creating time sheets, managing employees when they were on her shift, and generally keeping the store running. Joe, 21, was a college student, who took a job in Marion's store for the summer when he was home from school.

Joe liked Marion. She seemed like a fair boss and, while demanding, never made him feel like he couldn't do the job. She never called him out in front of other employees for any mistakes he might make (and he didn't make many).

Marion liked Joe. She was his supervisor, but the two of them and others regularly ate lunch together in the store's break room. Lots of banter, idle chitchat, and general discussion about all sorts of innocuous things took place during lunch. It was a relaxing break, and then back to work.

Sometimes some of the staff would gather after work for drinks before they headed home. Marion and Joe would often join the group.

On one such occasion, it became clear to Joe and his coworkers that Marion had a bit more interest in Joe than as a colleague. She hadn't had more to drink than the others, but her comments quickly turned rather lascivious.

"Joe, c'mon, you're not dating anyone, are you?" she asked.

He ignored the comment. Marion then walked around behind Joe. She put her arms around his neck and her face next to his, and whispered loud enough for all assembled to hear, "I don't scare you, do I?"

Joe pulled away, and Marion sat back down. When it came time to leave, they paid the bill and left the restaurant. As they were standing in the parking lot, another coworker asked Marion, "Are you okay to drive?"

Marion responded, "I don't think so." Then she smiled at Joe and said, "I want Joe to take me home."

Joe laughed and said he couldn't, to which Marion responded, "C'mon, Joe, prove you're a real man."

If you were Joe, what would you do?

A Stand back and break into your best rendition of Aloe Blacc's "The Man," crooning, "I'm the man, I'm the man, I'm the man / Yes I am, yes I am, yes I am." Then walk off. (If you have a mic, you could drop it right there, right then.)

B Let a coworker intercede and drive Marion home.

C At work the next day, ask for a meeting with the store manager, Marion's boss. Request that your schedule be changed so that your hours and Marion's no longer overlap.

D Don't show up to work the next day. Call in and quit.

E Take Marion home.

While he might have had a delightful singing voice and the move might have cut the tension, breaking into song (A) was not Joe's best option. He needed the money from the job to help defray his college costs, so quitting (D) wouldn't have been optimal. Plus, it didn't seem fair that he should have to quit since he had done nothing wrong. Joe had no desire to take Marion home (E), nor did he think it would be appropriate.

In this case, two things did happen. A colleague drove Marion home (B) and Joe asked if his schedule could be changed (C). Both exhibited good etiquette—well, as good as might be hoped given the unfortunate situation Marion had created.

Now, Joe might have tried to discuss the issue with Marion first thing the following day. But she was his supervisor, and he felt that getting into a long discussion with her about how what she did was inappropriate might create tension between them. He also might have decided to tough it out and hope that a non-drinking Marion would not be difficult to work with. But the discomfort she created made him feel that it would be better not to work when she was on the schedule.

When talking to the manager, Marion's boss, Joe did have to provide some awkward detail about what happened, but his request for a schedule change was accommodated. If it hadn't been, he was prepared to cobble together some work for the rest of the summer somewhere else. And if the store manager believed that Marion's behavior crossed into harassment, it would be the manager's responsibility to address that behavior head-on.

Workplace romance is risky, even between consenting adults.

With workplace romances, remember the following:

> Don't use your position or rank to cajole someone into a relationship.
> If your company has a workplace romance policy, make sure not to violate it. If it's stupid, work on getting it changed before you enter into a workplace romance.
> Keep your romance out of the office.
> Do not let talk of your romance interfere with getting your job done.
> If you break off a romance, be professional. Do not use your coworkers as relationship counselors.
> Refrain from drinking too much around coworkers. (Should you find that you did drink too much, call an Uber.)
> Get out more. Meet new people. But if you must fall in love with someone at work, don't be a jerk about it. Romance should be a good thing, not one that harms you, your romancer, your coworkers, your supervisor, or anyone else at work.

BULLY
FOR YOU

DIFFICULT
COLLEAGUES

W hat kind of difficult colleague are you? The question reads like a BuzzFeed quiz, doesn't it? Show me some pictures of dessert toppings and slingback pumps to choose from and bada bing, the BuzzFeed algorithm will determine exactly what type of difficult employee I am. The challenge for you, however, is to know how to deal with me, the difficult colleague, without turning into one yourself in the process.

Part of the problem is that few managers are willing to deal directly with difficult colleagues until their behavior becomes so disruptive that it's impossible to avoid. We're not talking poor performers here. Those, too, are often ignored by managers to the detriment of the business and its employees, but some of them are likeable enough.

Difficult colleagues can be productive. They're just painful to deal with. They might be loud, monopolizing every meeting. They might be arrogant know-it-alls, leaving little room for others to have an opinion, contribute ideas, or do their own work without judgment. Their behavior can sometimes be downright bullying if they're determined to get their own way.

Hoping they will disappear is not a strategy. The challenge is learning to manage them so you can get your work done without dealing with the difficult side of the colleague any more than you have to. Having the patience to do so is where etiquette comes in.

Tim was loud. Tim was smart. Tim knew how to get the resources he needed to get projects funded. Tim behaved as though he was the smartest person in the room—or, more often than not, as though he was the only smart person in the room. His colleagues couldn't stand working with him.

But Tim was productive. Tim pleased the clients with his performance. And Tim refused to share any credit with others even when credit was due. His colleagues loathed him.

Tim managed up. He worked well with the boss and even let the boss talk when everyone was together at meetings. The boss saw how Tim was productive, well-liked by customers, and resourceful in getting his job done. But as soon as the boss wasn't around, Tim was demanding, judgmental, dismissive, and impatient. His colleagues would have liked to see him go.

But it became clear that Tim wasn't going anywhere. So Tim's colleagues had to figure out a way to rein in his behavior and still get their own jobs done.

If you were Tim's colleague, what would your strategy be?

A At every meeting, allot some "Tim time." Some of Tim's behavior comes from his need to feel heard, so ask him direct questions and let him answer. But keep the questions focused.

B Whenever possible, do not let Tim be the last person to lay hands on reports before they go to the boss or to a client. That way, he can't take full credit for them.

C Whenever Tim is critical, ask him why he thinks the way he does. Ask him for suggestions, but don't engage in any arguing.

D If Tim's behavior ever comes too close to outright bullying, take him aside and tell him he's stepped over a line, and that while his opinion is valued, bullying is unacceptable.

E In whatever approach you take to work with and manage Tim, do not become Tim.

While none of these options is a foolproof strategy, Tim's colleagues chose A, B, C, D, and E as their solutions to the challenge. (Difficult colleagues often call for more than one strategy. Truly difficult colleagues may require more than five.)

The overall strategy was to minimize disruptions and maximize whatever value Tim might bring to the tasks at hand. It wouldn't always work. Tim would continue to bulldoze his way over everyone except the boss sometimes. But if their strategy was going to have a chance of working, Tim's colleagues couldn't expect miracles overnight. When you're learning to manage difficult colleagues, it can take months and sometimes years to see results.

I know, I know. *They're* the difficult ones. Why should *you* have to take the time to manage them? Because you're not the difficult one. You are a reasonable, productive, civil colleague who wants to do good work and get the best work out of others. Just because Tim is a difficult colleague, don't assume that you have to become a difficult colleague as well to take him on. Draw the line at bullying. Focus on the work to be done, not on how annoying your Tim is.

Employees regularly complain that management does little to address problem colleagues in the workplace. Don't expect to go your entire work life without experiencing a challenging colleague. And don't become one yourself.

Be the better person.

If you must deal with difficult colleagues, remember these rules:

> Figure out how to listen to them and let them know you're listening. Sort out the bluster from the useful information.

> Don't engage in behavior similar to the difficult colleague's. Getting into an argument with someone who lives to argue is a no-win time suck and doesn't solve the problem.

> Whenever possible, don't let your Tim be in a position to have the final say on a project or proposal. Make sure that everyone gets proper credit. But give your Tim the credit he deserves, too, even if he is a walking ball of pain. Be the better person.

> Make a pact with colleagues (not the difficult ones) to tell each other if you begin to behave like your office Tim. You do not want to be your office Tim. You're better than that.

SPEAK YOUR PIECE TO KEEP THE PEACE

INTERPERSONAL CONFLICTS

The best way to handle workplace conflicts is to avoid them, or at least not exacerbate them. Your work colleagues are not your children. You are neither tasked with rearing them nor teaching them manners. Thinking you can change how others behave is both arrogant and a fool's errand.

But even with the people you're closest to at work, even among those with whom you work best, conflicts are bound to arise. Learning to manage such conflicts so they don't grow into full-blown battles or "dead to me" proclamations is critical for anyone who wants to survive in the workplace and not let conflicts get in the way of doing good work.

Walker was a great colleague. When Frank joined the firm a couple of years ago, Walker was the first one to offer to show him around and introduce him to others in the office. When the boss put them on the same team, Walker always pulled his weight and was quick to give Frank and others the credit they deserved.

But Walker had an annoying habit of giving his coworkers nicknames, even if the targets found them off-putting or offensive. "All in good fun," Walker would respond. Or, "But it fits you so well!"

"Thunderbolt!" Walker called the company's CFO, Lindsay. "Green Bean!" was his nickname for Hugh, the communications head. "Big O!" he'd call Ted O'Brien, a bookkeeper in accounting. The CIO, Cary, was "Ball of Confusion."

Walker liked to call Frank "Sabertooth." Frank suspected that it had something to do with his overbite, his ability to close deals, or something else known only to Walker's imagination. Frank hated the nickname. He wanted Walker to stop calling him Sabertooth, particularly when they met with clients or prospective clients.

Frank had asked Walker if he could stop calling him by his nickname once in the past, but Walker just said, "All in good fun, Sabertooth. All in good fun."

Frank suspected that others in the company hated the nicknames Walker made up for them, too. He thought it was childish and often embarrassing. But he didn't want to jeopardize his working relationship with Walker by escalating the issue. Still, he wanted him to stop.

What would you do in Frank's situation?

A Punch Walker on the nose next time he calls you Sabertooth, mutter, "How's that for all in good fun?" and walk away.

B E-mail each of the colleagues you know Walker has nicknames for, ask them if they would like Walker to stop, then print out the responses and take them to Walker as evidence that he is driving people nuts.

C E-mail other colleagues with nicknames, but instead of bringing the printouts to Walker, take them to HR and ask them to have a sit-down with Walker.

D   Tell Walker again that you would prefer him not to use a nickname for you. If he jokes in response, tell him that you're serious. You really find the nickname uncomfortable and would like Walker to stop.

E   Decide that the issue is not big enough to jeopardize your working relationship with Walker over it. Sometimes you need to decide which issues are big enough to fall on your sword over, and this is not one.

Never punch anyone in the workplace (A). Never. Well, I take that back. If you believe your life or someone else's is in jeopardy, and you believe punching someone on the nose might help save a life, go right ahead and do it. Nicknames are not life-threatening, so no punching in this instance.

Collecting information on people's reactions to nicknames and presenting them to Walker (B) or HR (C) might be tempting. But you'd want to inform the people responding to your e-mail that you plan to make their responses known. Even then, using others to try to get Walker to change something that you personally find annoying is not as direct an approach as dealing with the issue yourself.

E is a reasonable option. Frank could ask himself if the conflict over the nickname-calling was great enough to risk his working relationship with Walker. Sometimes, learning to live with others' quirks is okay. But if that quirk got in the way of Frank doing his job or prevented Walker and Frank from working well together with clients, then Frank had no choice but to talk to Walker directly about cutting it out.

The nickname really did bother Frank, so he decided to talk with Walker again (D). He prefaced the conversation by reminding Walker how much he liked to work with him and that he appreciated how welcoming Walker had been to him at the company. Then he said that he would like the nickname-calling to stop. He made it clear that he was serious and that he found the nickname truly distracting and inappropriate. As Frank learned, dealing directly with the person with whom you have a conflict is often the best first approach.

Deal with conflicts calmly and directly.

Here's what to do when you're dealing with interpersonal conflicts at work:

> Take a deep breath before attacking the issue head on. Letting things cool off rather than escalate often proves more fruitful.

> Do not spread gossip about the person with whom you're having a conflict. If you spread enough gossip, you can become a bigger problem than the one you're trying to solve, and you'll end up looking like the bigger jerk in the process.

> Don't try to change your coworkers' personal behavior or mannerisms. That's neither appropriate nor your job.

> Decide if the conflict gets in the way of your working together. If so, consider talking to the person directly. If not, consider letting it go.

> Don't ever become the person you swore you'd never become. Show integrity rather than fighting dirty by spreading gossip or trapping a coworker to win a dispute.

> If the conflict gets in the way of work, deal with it as directly as possible, even if that means finding a way to be reassigned from working with this colleague.

> Be patient. Don't escalate. Don't be a jerk. Be the better person.

WHEN BAD BOSSES HAPPEN TO GOOD PEOPLE

DISPUTES WITH MANAGEMENT

W hen you find yourself in times of trouble, Mother Mary comes to . . . Sorry, wrong verse. When you find yourself in times of trouble at work, and that trouble involves management, what do you do?

In a curious flare-up, a boss named Andre instituted some changes in the department, which he believed to be good (and which mostly were). One of his managers, Leland, was disappointed (okay, pissed) that Andre hadn't consulted with him or other managers before trying to institute the changes.

Andre, who was relatively new to the position, wanted to make sure that the changes would happen, so he presented them to his bosses without indicating that he hadn't sought anyone else's input, including his managers'. Andre was not obligated to consult with his managers. He could present any plan he wanted to present. But while the results were overall positive for employees, they resulted in more work and less net compensation for managers like Leland. If Andre expected his managers to buy into the changes, it might have made sense to consult with them first.

Leland raised the issue with Andre's bosses and indicated that he would like to step down as department manager. In response, one of the boss's bosses called Leland and offered him an increase in salary to compensate for the way the situation was handled. Leland thanked him and told him he would think about the offer.

But the next morning, Catherine, another of Andre's bosses, asked for a meeting with Leland. At the meeting, Catherine told Leland that they could not increase his compensation after all. She did offer instead to put more money into his research budget, but the increased salary was a no-go.

Leland, who hadn't asked for more money in the first place, felt a bit whipsawed. An offer made by one boss was rescinded the next day by another? He told Catherine that he was disappointed that the company's management would go back on its word. She responded that she understood, but that she had experienced such disappointments throughout her career and she got over it. Besides, the research money indicated how much Leland meant to the company.

Leland felt lied to and disappointed. Still, he had to decide how to proceed. What would you do in his shoes?

Ⓐ Tell Catherine that her tales of personal dissatisfaction mean nothing to you, quit on the spot, and slam the door on the way out of her office.

Ⓑ Go back to your office and type a detailed letter in which you lay out how you've been lied to, who lied to you, how your boss botched managing the division, how much you've contributed to the growth of your department, and how the original commitment to give you a raise must be honored.

C Calmly tell Catherine you're disappointed and ask if she's certain that they won't be willing to honor the original offer. Thank her for making the effort to show how the company values your work by offering you more research funds.

D Begin to look for a new job elsewhere.

E Tell every member of your department what happened and caution them to take anything Andre says with a grain of salt.

While option A might feel good in the heat of the moment, it would not get Catherine to change her mind, nor would it remove Andre from his position. Instead, Leland would be out of work and unlikely to get a good reference from his prior employer. It would also be bad etiquette to slam doors. The door had done nothing to Leland.

Writing a scathing letter explaining why Andre was wrong in excruciating detail (B) would not have been without value. The value would be in *writing* the letter, however, not in sending it. A letter written in anger and sent to management is rarely a good idea. Too often, such letters come back to haunt their writers. In this case, it would more than likely make management think of Leland as a hothead who couldn't control his emotions. Control your emotions if you want to get something done.

You know where I stand on gossip: It's never good. Spreading gossip to your own employees (E) is a terrible idea. Why would employees trust a manager who gossips about others not to gossip about them? Gossip will do you harm more often than it will do you good.

Leland chose option C. He calmly asked Catherine if she was certain they couldn't reinstate the offer that was made and acknowledged the effort she'd made to do something positive with the research budget. This choice was professional and gracious, and it accomplished about as much as he could hope to accomplish in such a botched situation.

But given the way the situation was handled, there would be nothing wrong with Leland seeing if he could find a new job in an environment more to his liking (D). Of course, that's always a crapshoot; similar situations might crop up with management at a new place of employment. New opportunities often seem better until they're no longer new.

Do not go all Jerry Maguire.

If you find yourself in a dispute with management, here are some things to keep in mind:

> Try to stay calm.
> Do not go all Jerry Maguire and write a manifesto to management airing how you've been wronged and what must be done to make you whole.
> Ask questions to see if you can resolve the conflict in a way that comes close to being palatable.
> Don't threaten to quit as a leveraging tool. Threatening others is never a sure thing.
> If you do suggest you might quit, be prepared to be separated from your company.
> Ask yourself how hard you want to fight to get the conflict resolved exactly how you want it to be resolved. Don't expect to be able to fall on your sword over and over again and come out unscathed.
> Do not engage in gossip to try to get other employees to side with you.
> Decide if the conflict is enough to make you want to work someplace else. If it is, begin a thoughtful job search.

HAVE BUSINESS, WILL TRAVEL

TRAVELING FOR WORK

In the late 1990s, I wrote a column for *Inc.* magazine called "The Road Warrior." The mission of the column was to send me on the road with some sort of new technology to see how well it worked. At times, it seemed more as if I was tasked with breaking something—getting lost when using some early GPS technology in rental cars or calling a computer company in Munich to try to find a charger for a laptop when all the voicemail choices were in German and the extent of my German was President John F. Kennedy's "Ich bin ein Berliner" speech.

But the experience of writing the column had me on the road for work quite a bit. What made this a particularly interesting experience for me is that I'm not a fan of flying or of sleeping in anything other than my own bed. (Okay, I'll admit that a wicker couch on a screened porch makes for a good nap.) I was also never comfortable combining business and personal travel. The two are distinctly different. When traveling for business, it's important to remember that the primary purpose isn't relaxation or getting away, it's achieving a goal for business. Whether it's research, sales, or something else, the focus during business travel should always remain on the task at hand.

You're representing yourself while traveling for business, but you're also representing your company. (If you're self-employed, there's no difference.) When you're traveling for pleasure, you might spend the entire time in cargo shorts and flip-flops. Such attire would rarely be appropriate when traveling for business, unless, of course, you were selling cargo shorts and flip-flops or filming a series of videos on the wildest flip-flop beaches in the world.

You should keep thorough records when traveling for business. If you're being reimbursed for your expenses, make sure to keep close track of them. Never try to pad your expense report. It's dishonest and also pretty tacky to do so. (I once worked with a guy who tried to get someone to say she had been at a dinner with him so he could pad his expense account for more than the company's per diem allowed. Dishonest. Tacky. She said no.)

One challenge when you're traveling abroad is to gauge appropriate behavior. If you're out to dinner and at a loss about what to do with all the cutlery surrounding your dinner plate, follow your host's lead. Some basic rules you learned (or should have learned) at home still apply: Don't tuck your napkin into your shirt collar or use your knife to eat peas. In other words, show some class, for Pete's sake!

On a business trip to Belgium, a young businessperson named Pauline found herself invited to a formal dinner with several hundred guests. The setting was a several-hundred-year-old castle-like building. Lots of gilt and glittering chandeliers.

Pauline had never been to such a formal dinner before, but fortunately she'd been told before she left home to pack appropriate clothing, which she did. She was the lone American at a table of about 10 Belgians.

Drinks were served: sweet wine, which she sipped, but never would have ordered on her own, and Belgian beer, which she rather liked. The conversation was easy with the clients and prospective clients at the table. They spoke English fluently, which made up for her inability to speak their native language. She stayed away from discussing politics or religion at the table, something she remembered her parents advising her to do if she didn't know her dinner companions well.

A small salad arrived. She saw one of the guests at her table use his salad fork, so she used her own. The salad plates were cleared and the appetizer was served: cooked eel with the spine still attached.

Pauline could smell it before it reached the table, and when it did arrive, it looked to her like a cross between a boiled snake and an overgrown worm. She had no idea how to eat it, whether to eat the spine, or which utensils to eat it with. Her confusion was accompanied by a waft of nausea at the thought of eating what was before her, something that she only knew was an eel because a guest at her table had said, "Oh, here comes the eel," when he saw the servers scurrying about.

What would you do when confronted with an eel?

A Excuse yourself from the table, sneak into the restroom to take out your smartphone, hail an Uber, and flee the premises.

B Excuse yourself from the table, sneak into the restroom to take out your smartphone, and Google information on how to eat spine-in eel in Brussels.

C Watch as others at the table eat their eel and then try a bit, feeling no obligation to clean your plate.

D Quickly change the conversation to politics, hoping that yelling will ensue and the entire table of guests will be asked to vacate the premises.

E Pick up the eel by the tail, dangle it over your mouth, and mutter, "Here fishy, fishy," before downing the whole thing.

A disappearing act (A) might have been tempting, but this wasn't some blind date gone bad. It was a business dinner. Being swooped away by a gallant Uber driver might rid Pauline of the need to figure out how to eat the eel, but it would leave the other guests wondering what happened to her. Calls would be made. Questions would be asked. Embarrassments would be had. Plus, it's just plain rude to abandon your business dinner companions.

Dangling the eel over her head (E)? While doing so might show spunk, save the spunk for those college reunions and family gatherings where it's expected of you. It's bad form while traveling for business.

Getting the whole table kicked out (D) might have been a bonding experience, but it is a lousy idea and risky to boot. No eel is worth creating such a ruckus.

Watching to see how others eat their eel (C) was the right etiquette, and that's what Pauline did. When in doubt while traveling, follow the locals' lead. If others pass on eating entirely, you might decide to do so yourself. But watching to see what utensil to use and then following suit is the right move here. It is also perfectly fine to admit that you've never eaten eel before and ask advice from your dinner companions. Seeking wisdom from your smartphone (B) is a spirited idea if you can truly do so discreetly, although the eel appetizer might be gone by the time you return from the restroom—perhaps a desired outcome, but then, leaving the table for too long is just plain rude.

Follow the locals' lead.

When traveling for business, consider the following:

> Don't dress like a slob. If you know ahead of time what sort of events you'll be attending, pack accordingly.

> Show up when and where you committed to showing up. Even if it's accepted practice at your company to show up 10 minutes late to meetings, don't expect that to be acceptable when traveling for business. Be on time.

> Follow the lead of the locals. When in doubt, watch how your local business contact conducts himself or herself, and follow suit.

> Don't be rude while traveling for business. But that goes for when you're not traveling for business as well.

> Keep good records of your expenses.

> Don't pad your expense account.

> Bring cash (in local currency, if necessary) in case credit cards are not accepted.

> Pack light, but be prepared for the events you know are scheduled.

> Don't treat a business trip like an all-expenses-paid vacation.

HOW DARE YOU TRY TO FACILITATE ME

CULTURAL SENSITIVITIES

About 15 years ago, I wrote a column about how tricky bribes can be. The tricky part, I noted then, was "deciding what constitutes a bribe and then whether you should pay one to do business in a foreign country—knowing full well that if you don't, a less ethical competitor might."

With the Foreign Corrupt Practices Act, Congress made it illegal to pay bribes to win foreign contracts. But by permitting "facilitating fees" and other options to expedite "routine government action," they left enough ambiguity to allow for practices that were deemed acceptable in foreign countries.

Some experts observed to me that it was obvious what crossed the line from a facilitating fee to an outright bribe. To others, facilitating payments were just bribes by another name.

I liked then and still like the advice offered by former Harvard Business School professor Walter Kuemmerle, who told me that "it's generally better to stay out of corruption processes for good than to go into them just tentatively." He added that if a "business decides to give in once . . . that strategy is definitely not going to work." Kuemmerle likened it to "a drug addiction. Once you signal that you're willing to play the game according to the local rules, it's very hard to reverse that policy."

Years ago, Dr. Geert Hofstede, a Dutch social psychologist, did research into different countries' cultures while working at IBM. The basics of his research, available widely online, detail differences in business etiquette among several different countries. It's too simplistic to assume that you can look at the work of researchers like Hoftstede and come away equipped to navigate the varied nuances of any culture. Still, such research points out that it's important to understand that there are differences in customs among various countries. You may be going into a business relationship with a company from a culture where what's deemed acceptable is different from what your own culture deems acceptable.

Being sensitive to cultural differences can be a challenging facet of business etiquette, but it's an important one, both to do business successfully and to avoid insulting people. A good rule of thumb is to never let a foreign culture's customs give you permission to break your own domestic laws. Just as you should be sensitive to other cultures, so too should others be sensitive to yours and the laws that guide you.

Diane was a manager at a midsize publishing company in the northeastern United States. She had worked for many years to build her division, which published college textbooks and online ancillaries aimed at the college market.

One afternoon, she received an e-mail from her boss asking her if she would be willing to make a presentation to a visiting delegation of businessmen and women from China. The group and a translator would be visiting various companies and organizations in the United States in what they were calling a "benchmark tour of best practices." Diane agreed to meet with the delegation.

When the meeting time arrived, the group was already assembled in a small conference room where Diane greeted each of them. The translator helped introduce each of the contingent's members to Diane. As they were introduced, each member of the group stood up to offer Diane a business card. Diane's boss had tipped her off that there would likely be a vigorous exchange of business cards, so she'd brought a small pile of her own to trade.

Diane was the only one in the room from her company. She made her presentation about the company's products and markets, highlighting details from their forthcoming line of new products. When she was through, she asked if anyone had any questions. A few questions came her way, which she seemed to answer to the group's satisfaction.

As they were finishing up, Diane thanked the group for their attention. The translator then chimed in: "Our group would like to offer you a small token of its appreciation for the time you took with us today."

With that announcement, one of the Chinese businessmen stood up, reached into his briefcase, and pulled out a wrapped package. He walked over to Diane and handed it to her, saying in English, "Thank you very much for your time."

Diane's company had a policy about giving and receiving gifts from vendors. Such gifts could not have a value of more than $50, and they had to be reported to the company.

On being handed the wrapped package from the Chinese contingent, what would you do?

A Rip off the wrapping paper, assess its worth by Googling comparable items on your smartphone, and then decide if you should keep it or not.

B Take it and sell whatever it is on eBay, figuring that these guys are not vendors, and since no one else from the company is in the room, who will know?

C Accept the gift, thank the contingent, and report the gift to your boss. Later, upon opening the gift, determine if it must be returned.

D Shake the gift a bit and make a comment to the effect of "I hope it's chocolates. I love chocolates."

E Refuse to take the gift and announce in a clearly agitated voice, "How dare you try to bribe me?" then storm from the room.

Researching the gift's value online in front of your guests (A) is gauche in just about any culture. It would have been both rude and insulting to those making the gesture. It may have been technically correct to sell the item without reporting it (B) because the people in this group were not vendors and therefore weren't covered by her company's gift policy, but doing so would violate the spirit if not the letter of the policy. Hoping for chocolates (D) might get a laugh among Diane's friends at a gift swap, but it would have shown little appreciation or sensitivity to a group of visiting businesspeople she'd just met. Free-floating outrage and indignation (E) might be a good release during particularly intense quarters, but if that's what was going on here, then a good run at lunchtime would be a better choice. There was no indication that the group was asking her to do anything and no suggestion that a bribe was being made, so a rush to judgment would have been silly.

Accepting the gift, reporting it, and determining if it ran afoul of the company's gift policy after the group had left (C) showed the most grace and sensitivity, and Diane chose it as the most appropriate response. Given that the contingent had been traveling throughout the United States before their meeting with Diane, it was very likely that they were familiar with what was acceptable in terms of gift giving. While, culturally, it might be important to the group to express their thanks with a gift, they could do so and still be sensitive to Diane's own cultural norms.

Never let a foreign culture's customs give you permission to break your own domestic laws.

Here are some things to remember before engaging in business with those whose cultural norms may be different from your own:

> Be patient if others' norms don't mirror your own.

> Do some research on what to expect. Look for the most current information available online and in print. (Fons Trompenaars and Charles Hampden-Turner's *Riding the Waves of Culture: Understanding Diversity in Global Business* is as good a place as any to start.)

> Never break your own laws, regulations, or policies to service what you believe to be someone else's cultural norms.

> Consult with others who have done a significant amount of business with the culture in question to see if they can offer any insight.

> While it is likely that people from other cultures might have familiarized themselves with your cultural norms, don't assume this to be the case.

> Do not be insulted if someone's behavior seems foreign to your way of doing business.

> If something gives you pause during a business meeting, consult with others at your company to assess if there's an issue or if a misunderstanding needs to be addressed.

> But mostly, be patient if others' norms don't mirror your own.

ASK A BOSS

WHAT'S THE BEST OR WORST BEHAVIOR YOU'VE SEEN AT A COMPANY SOCIAL FUNCTION?

MarketingProfs is a virtual company, so Ann Handley, its chief content officer, says that "getting together in person is always a blast." The company looks for ways in which employees can "hang informally," like throwing pizza parties in a hotel's presidential suite, zip-lining in Las Vegas, and biking to a winery for a wine tasting in Cape May, New Jersey. (All fun and good, but I've always been curious about the wisdom of wine tasting while on bicycles, even though I know it's a thing.) "We just try to have fun and relax," writes Handley about her virtual company's culture. "We've found that not having corporate-ish events brings out the best in people."

The best behavior Sam Baber, director of talent and development at Spredfast, has seen is when the company's CEO stood at the entrance for the first two hours of a party to welcome every employee and his or her significant other. The worst? "The following holiday party, there was a new CEO. When people showed up they saw no leader in sight, only to find the CEO upstairs in a corner not interacting with the rest of the employees."

Dave Hills, the CEO of Twelvefold, says that at a holiday party, just before an announcement was to be made about her promotion to CEO, an employee "had a few drinks and then decided she'd engage the chairman of the company in a discussion about what she thought was wrong with the operations of the company." While Hills reports that no one heard the exact conversation, "the result of it was she announced her retirement a week or so after the party."

What's the worst behavior that Dean Miller, Connecticut Public Broadcasting's senior vice president of content, has seen? "A tantrum over not receiving an expected company-wide award."

Office Jargon (and What It Really Means)

Here are 15 phrases that are commonly used in business but do not generally mean what you think they mean. In fact, they sometimes mean something else entirely.

OFFICE JARGON	TRANSLATION
"I'll call you sometime," said after a random encounter with an acquaintance you met once at a party or conference.	"I'll not be calling you anytime soon, maybe never."
"That's an interesting question," said in response to a question you raise at a meeting or in an interview.	"That's one of the lamest questions I've ever heard, but give me a moment to compose myself and answer you in a gracious manner."
"We have plans for you."	"We haven't a clue what to do with you or about you or for you. If we did, we'd have told you."
"Why did you choose to leave your last job?"	"I'm asking this during an interview as a subterfuge to see if you'll trash your former employer." Don't fall for it. Focus on why you're interested in the new job and what you'd bring to the new company. Refrain from bad-mouthing former employers or colleagues.

OFFICE JARGON	TRANSLATION
"He's not a team player."	The manager who says this didn't get his way and is throwing one of his employees to the wolves for not getting on board with his way, regardless of how inane his way might have been.
"Are you sure you want to take a chance on someone like him?"	Too often, this means "People who aren't like me are not to be trusted or are always causing trouble." It can be a cover for sexism, racism, religious bigotry, and all sorts of nastiness. Avoid falling prey to such observations. Don't let others asking such questions make you question your own judgment or turn you into them. Feel free to be judgmental about bigots.
"So and so is not without talent."	"He's not very good."
"We'd love to do more, but the budget just won't allow it."	Others probably got a better raise than you did.
"Please e-mail me the details; that way I won't forget to follow up."	"Please, please, please forget to e-mail me, so it becomes your fault I don't follow up."
"I'm not a details person."	"You're going to end up doing all the work."
"I never listen to my voicemail anymore."	"I never listen to the voicemails you leave me anymore."
"Can we backburner this for a bit?"	"Your idea will never see the light of day again."
"Stay tuned."	"I haven't finished the assignment. I don't know when I will finish the assignment. Don't count on me finishing the assignment. But stay tuned."

OFFICE JARGON	TRANSLATION
"I was hoping you could spend some time talking with me about your business."	"Please offer me a job."
"I enjoyed the work you did on so-and-so."	"I just Googled you and found that you worked on so-and-so. I have no idea what so-and-so is or what you did on it. I want you to think I'm curious and resourceful. I want you to really, really like me."

References

Atlassian. "You Waste a Lot of Time at Work." Atlassian.com. Accessed September 23, 2015. www.atlassian.com/time-wasting-at-work-infographic.

Backstrom, Lars, Paolo Boldi, Marco Rosa, Johan Ugander, and Sebastiano Vigna. "Four Degrees of Separation." January 6, 2012. arxiv.org/pdf /1111.4570v3.pdf.

Beacon staff. "Cartoon Discussed at Forum." *The Berkeley Beacon.* March 1, 2006. www.berkeleybeacon.com/news/2006/3/1/cartoon-discussed-at -forum.

Broderick, Ryan, and Emanuella Grinberg. "10 People Who Learned Social Media Can Get You Fired." BuzzFeed/CNN. CNN.com. Last modified June 6, 2013. www.cnn.com/2013/06/06/living/buzzfeed-social-media-fired/.

Clinton, Hillary Rodham. "Putting the Elements of Smart Power into Practice." U.S. Department of State. February 19, 2009. www.state.gov /secretary/20092013clinton/rm/2009a/02/119411.htm.

Coutu, Diane. "Why Teams Don't Work." *Harvard Business Review.* May 2009. www.hbr.org/2009/05/why-teams-dont-work.

Grant, Adam. "Friends at Work? Not So Much." *The New York Times.* September 4, 2015. www.nytimes.com/2015/09/06/opinion/sunday /adam-grant-friends-at-work-not-so-much.html.

Hackman, J. Richard, *Leading Teams: Setting the Stage for Great Performances.* Boston: Harvard Business Review Press, 2002.

Hall, Edward T. *The Hidden Dimension.* New York: Anchor Books, 1990.

Halper, Katie, "A Brief History of People Getting Fired for Social Media Stupidity." *Rolling Stone.* July 13, 2015. www.rollingstone.com/culture/lists /a-brief-history-of-people-getting-fired-for-social-media-stupidity -20150713.

Hofstede, Geert, Gert Jan Hofstede, and Michael Minkov. *Cultures and Organizations: Software of the Mind,* Third Edition. New York: McGraw-Hill, 2010.

Jones, Robin. "Top Office Etiquette Rules: Pay Attention, and Be Nice." Accountemps. RobertHalf.com. May 26, 2015. www.roberthalf.com /accountemps/blog/top-office-etiquette-rules-pay-attention-and-be-nice.

Kidder, Tracy. *Mountains Beyond Mountains*. New York: Random House, 2003.

Martin, Kingsley. "Winston Churchill Interviewed in 1939: 'The British People Would Rather Go Down Fighting.'" *The New Statesman*. NewStatesman.com. January 6, 2014. www.newstatesman.com/archive/2013/12/british-people -would-rather-go-down-fighting.

Mercer, David. "State Lateness 'Costs the Economy £9 Billion Every Year.'" *The Independent*. Independent.com. September 30, 2012. www.independent.co .uk/news/business/news/staff-lateness-costs-the-economy-9-billion-every -year-8191289.html.

Proskauer Rose. "Social Media in the Workplace Around the World 3.0." Proskauer.com. Accessed September 24, 2015. www.proskauer.com/files /uploads/social-media-in-the-workplace-2014.pdf.

Radicati, Sara. "Email Statistics Report, 2014–2018." Radicati.com. www.radicati.com/wp/wp-content/uploads/2014/01/Email-Statistics -Report-2014-2018-Executive-Summary.pdf.

Riordan, Christine M., and Rodger W. Griffeth. "The Opportunity for Friendship in the Workplace: An Underexplored Construct." *Journal of Business and Psychology* 10, no. 2 (December 1995): 141–54.

"SAI Global Compliance Survey of Gift Policies Finds Most Organizations Mandate Employee Reporting Exceptions to Gift Policies Seldom if Ever Granted." BusinessWire.com. December 19, 2013. www.businesswire.com /news/home/20131219005299/en/SAI-Global-Compliance-Survey-Gift -Policies-Finds#.VgOMH3t2nqQ.

Seglin, Jeffrey L. "Between Consenting Co-Workers." The Right Thing, *New York Times*. September 20, 1998. www.nytimes.com/1998/09/20 /business/the-right-thing-between-consenting-co-workers.html.

———. "Boundaries to Stealing All Those Bright Ideas." The Right Thing, *New York Times*. January 17, 1999. www.nytimes.com/1999/01/17 /business/the-right-thing-boundaries-to-stealing-all-those-bright -ideas.html.

———. "In Ethics, It's The Thought That Counts." The Right Thing, *New York Times*. December 19, 1999. www.nytimes.com/1999/12/19/business /the-right-thing-in-ethics-it-s-the-thought-that-counts.html.

————. *The Good, the Bad, and Your Business: Choosing Right When Ethical Dilemmas Pull You Apart.* Kittery Point, ME: Smith/Kerr, 2007.

————. *The Right Thing: Conscience, Profit and Personal Responsibility in Today's Business.* Kittery Point, ME: Smith/Kerr, 2006.

————. "Rudeness Makes Dinner Invite Tasteless." *Chicago Tribune.* April 22, 2014. articles.chicagotribune.com/2014-04-22/entertainment /sns-201404221300--tms--ritethngctnrt-a20140422-20140422_1_dinner -invite-companies-esops.

————. "Telling the Truth, or at Least Most of It." The Right Thing, *New York Times.* May 21, 2000. www.nytimes.com/2000/05/21/business /the-right-thing-telling-the-truth-or-at-least-most-of-it.html.

————. "We've Got to Start Meeting Like This." *CIO.* March 31, 2001.

————. "When Bribery Is Lost in Translation." The Right Thing, *New York Times.* October 15, 2000. www.nytimes.com/2000/10/15/business /the-right-thing-when-bribery-is-lost-in-translation.html.

————. "You've Got Mail. You're Being Watched." The Right Thing, *New York Times.* July 18, 1999. www.nytimes.com/1999/07/18/business /the-right-thing-you-ve-got-mail-you-re-being-watched.html.

————. and Edward Coleman. *The AMA Handbook of Business Letters,* 4th Ed. New York: AMACOM, 2012.

Society for Human Resource Management. "SHRM Survey Findings: Workplace Romance." SHRM.org. September 24, 2013. www.shrm.org /research/surveyfindings/articles/pages/shrm-workplace-romance -findings.aspx.

Stillman, Jessica. "Want More Creative Meetings? Try Standing Up." Inc.com. June 19, 2014. www.inc.com/jessica-stillman/want-more-creative-meetings -stand-up.html.

Trompenaars, Fons, and Charles Hampden-Turner. *Riding the Waves of Culture: Understanding Diversity in Global Business.* New York: McGraw-Hill, 2012.

Index

CPSIA information can be obtained at www.ICGtesting.com
Printed in the USA
BVOW11s0446261215

430975BV00020B/83/P